WITHIN
OUR
MEANS

WITHIN
OUR
MEANS

*The Struggle
for Economic Recovery
After
a Reckless Decade*

ALFRED L. MALABRE, JR.

RANDOM HOUSE NEW YORK

Grateful acknowledgment is made to the following for permission to reprint previously published material:

THE CONFERENCE BOARD, INC.: Excerpts from "Productivity Needs of the United States," Research Report No. 934, by Audrey Freedman. Published by The Conference Board, Inc. Reprinted by permission.

THE NEW YORK TIMES: Excerpt from "Pro-Life? Then Pay Up" by Lloyd N. Cutler from the July 7, 1989, issue of *The New York Times.* Copyright © 1989 by The New York Times Company. Reprinted by permission.

THE WALL STREET JOURNAL: Excerpts from "A National Savings President" by Martin Feldstein from the November 21, 1988, issue of *The Wall Street Journal;* excerpt from "Why the Twin Deficits Are a Blessing" by Milton Friedman from the December 14, 1988, issue of *The Wall Street Journal.* Copyright © 1988. Reprinted by permission of *The Wall Street Journal.*

THE WASHINGTON POST: Excerpt from "Who Will Pay for Bush's Vision?" by Leon E. Panetta from the August 3, 1990, issue of *The Washington Post*. Copyright © 1990 The Washington Post. Reprinted by permission.

Library of Congress Cataloging-in-Publication Data

Malabre, Alfred L.
    Within our means: the struggle for economic recovery after a reckless
    decade / by Alfred L. Malabre, Jr.
        p.   cm.
    ISBN 0-394-57975-5
    1. United States—Economic policy—1981– 2. Finance, Public—
    United States. 3. United States—Commercial policy. I. Title.
    HC106.8.M319 1991   338.973′001′12—dc20   90—52706

Design by Robert Bull Design.

Manufactured in the United States of America

98765432

First Edition

In loving memory of my mother and my father

The probable economic winners of the Cold War are West Germany and Japan. The United States has been made into a second-class industrial economy with worse yet to come.

—SEYMOUR MELMAN, professor emeritus of industrial
engineering at Columbia University,
in *The New York Times*, June 3, 1990

FOREWORD

Much has happened since I started this book two years ago. A very large federal budget deficit, which had briefly begun to narrow, has recently resumed growing and become larger than ever. The economy's durable expansion, which had lasted more than twice as long as the average economic upturn, has now expired. Unemployment, which recently reached the lowest level in many years, is on the rise again. Inflation, which nearly disappeared after the 1981–82 recession, has once again intensified.

Abroad, the Soviet Union has changed remarkably from a threatening Communist monolith—Ronald Reagan's "evil empire"—to a troubled, fragmenting refugee from communism. Along with its former East European satellites, it struggles to shed a state-controlled economy for one that is market-driven. The two Germanys are in the process of reuniting. And elsewhere, in the wake of Iraq's invasion of Kuwait, a huge American military force sits in the Middle East, at a cost of more than $1 billion a month. Senator Sam Nunn, the Georgia Democrat who chairs the Senate Armed Services Committee, recently estimated that the expense of this buildup, plus other costs entailed in the blockade of Iraq, could come to $50 billion a year. And if a war breaks out, he added, the military cost alone could reach $1 billion a *day*.

Much more will surely change in coming months, but huge imponderables make it impossible to anticipate developments with any precision. At this writing, all sorts of crucial questions are unanswerable. Among them:

Will there be a protracted military standoff between Iraq and the United States and its allies? Will the sanctions work? If there is fighting, will the United States manage to bring down the Iraqi leadership swiftly, without major disruptions of oil production in the area? If there are disruptions, how high will the price of oil climb? Will it reach $50 or $60 a barrel, as some analysts fear? If it does reach such levels, how seriously will this affect the economies of the United States and other industrial nations? (The Joint Economic Committee of Congress recently estimated that each one-dollar increase in the price of a barrel of oil drains about $3 billion a year from America's gross national product.)

On the domestic front, will any real headway be made, through tax increases and spending cuts, toward reducing the budget deficit? If such measures are applied, as now seems likely, how will an economy already faltering respond to medicine normally prescribed only when business activity is expanding too rapidly and threatening to overheat, rather than cooling down? Will a recession produce massive failures among the countless businesses that are already staggering under record-heavy debt-service burdens?

The list of unanswerable questions goes on. Still, it seems clear that we Americans must face up at last to living within our means. That is my message in this book, and nothing likely to happen in coming months can change that situation. The jig is up. The gap between our behavior and our capabilities is no longer sustainable. Our only choice is whether to work to close the gap in an orderly manner and as painlessly as possible or to have the closing forced on us in painful ways by developments beyond our control.

With Operation Desert Shield in mind, Kevin Phillips, the author of *The Politics of Rich and Poor,* recently remarked that we tend to exhibit "imperial behavior without the imperial checkbook." Much the same may be said of our behavior in general. We continue to address ominous developments in a cavalier fashion. Debt continues to pile up in all sectors of the economy. There is increasing shakiness in such once-sound businesses as banking and insurance. The infrastructure continues to crumble, hampering gains in productivity. Meanwhile, top officials of the Bush administration have had to scour the globe in search of funds for Operation Desert Shield. This demeaning endeavor brings to mind a public television fund-raiser: Japan has just pledged $3 billion. Germany promises $2 billion. Be generous and give. Our operators are waiting to take your calls.

Thanks largely to huge loans from abroad and asset sales to foreign buyers, we have been able to spend excessively for many years—since long before the Bush team's telethon began for Desert Shield. But this comfortable arrangement is ending. Foreign purchases of American stocks and bonds, once in high demand abroad, are running far below the pace of a year or two ago. By no coincidence, the dollar, which weakened in the latter years of Reagan's presidency, is sagging further and inflation, with consumer prices rising at nearly 10 percent, cuts deeply into buying power. With all of this, surveys show the steepest decline in consumer confidence in more than a decade, since before the last recession.

As we look ahead, is it any wonder that so many of our young people are coming glumly to believe that theirs is the first generation of Americans whose standard of living will fall short of what their parents knew. Better than their parents, perhaps, they understand that the checkbook is impecunious, not imperial, that difficult adjustments must be made, and that whatever develops in coming months in the Middle East or Washington or elsewhere, we Americans must now begin, voluntarily or otherwise, to live within our means.

Quogue, N.Y.
September 1990

ACKNOWLEDGMENTS

Besides my wonderful word processor, there are several actual human beings I would like to thank for making this book possible—for their inspiration, patience, support, and crucial help when help was needed. They include Lindley Clark, my gentle, sagacious colleague at *The Wall Street Journal,* whose advice in matters pertaining to our poor overburdened economy is second to none; Michael Carlisle, my agent, whose enthusiasm is boundless and infectious; Jason Epstein, my editor, a word magician who commands my enduring gratitude and respect; and lastly but not leastly Mary Patricia Malabre, my benevolent spouse, who so generously read, urged, consoled, and cooked so deliciously.

CONTENTS

INTRODUCTION

F I V E years ago, I wrote a book called *Beyond Our Means,* whose title held a double meaning. As a nation, we Americans had been living beyond our means for a dangerously long while— for so long that it was beyond our means to set matters straight in a reasonably painless way. I was so bold as to forecast that America, overburdened by debt and without sufficient savings, investment, or productivity growth, was headed inexorably into difficult times.

The nature of the impending trouble, I submitted, could not be precisely gauged, but the likeliest course appeared to be sharply accelerating inflation or, alternatively, spreading deflation, accompanied in either case by increasing federal regulation of the economy in general and of financial institutions in particular. Ronald Reagan promised to get the government off our backs, but his legacy, ironically, would be a government that eventually weighed more heavily on our backs than ever before.

When I wrote *Beyond Our Means,* the federal debt was $1.8 trillion, which at the time seemed an awesome sum, twice the total of only a half decade earlier. But now that figure appears almost puny, for the amount the government owes is nearing $3.5 trillion. It seems likely to push above $4 trillion by 1993—$16,000 for every man, woman, and child—and servicing may well cost over $300 billion in yearly interest, matching recent Pentagon budgets. And beyond this pileup there lies the government's staggering financial obligation for the various agencies that it backs, a sum approximating $6 trillion, more than five times the size of recent federal budgets. And while this debt continues to mount—spurred ever higher by the burgeoning expense of turmoil in the Middle East and the savings-and-loan bailout—so does the share of the debt that's owed to foreigners. They hold some 20 percent of the federal debt, up from 15 percent in the mid-1980s, and one consequence is that more and more of the interest that American taxpayers must ultimately pay to service this debt winds up abroad—perhaps to be reinvested here, perhaps not. The latter eventuality would grow likelier, of course, with rising interest rates abroad and mounting capital needs in the newly democratic areas of Eastern Europe. This in turn would complicate the Treasury's borrowing, tending to force up interest rates and slow business activity in the United States.

For perspective, net interest on the federal debt consumes about 15 percent of all government spending. This exceeds, for instance, the combined amounts that the government spends on health, science, space, agriculture, housing, the protection of the environment, and the administration of justice. Entitlement programs and other mandatory spending take up another 48 percent of the budget and defense outlays another 25 percent. This leaves only some 12 percent, which includes aid to such important programs as education and drug treatment. Because efforts to hold down spending have been concentrated in these limited areas, the share of the budget they account for has fallen by two-thirds in the past decade.

The title of the book you are holding now, which is a sort of sequel to the earlier volume, also has two meanings. Nations and the people in them may live beyond their means for a considerable time—as we in America have clearly done—but sooner or later they must begin to live *within* their means. That time, for so long delayed, is at hand in America, I believe. But I also believe—this is the second meaning of the title—that it is within our means to restore our economy to reasonably sound health, though the task will entail some self-inflicted pain—higher taxes, less federal largess, tighter regulation of business activity. Especially painful is the prospect of higher taxes at the end of a prolonged economic expansion, when buying power is likely to be under increasing strain even without any tax rise. In other words, we

Americans are going to have to spend some serious time at the gym and less time at the dinner table.

We are already beginning to experience some of this pain—for example, in swiftly mounting state and local tax bills, with much more of this to come, I suspect. To continue avoiding the hard choices would ultimately entail far greater distress. We can set about living within our means in a purposeful way, with sensible programs and courageous leadership in Washington, or be dragged into it in humiliating fashion through the forces of an increasingly interdependent world economy. We have a choice: Either we make our own rules and live by them or let our creditors make the rules for us.

For a glimpse of the second possibility, consider what has befallen such once-profligate nations as Mexico and Brazil. Mexican living standards on the average have dropped by more than a third since the mid-1980s, surpassing even the slide in U.S. living standards during the Great Depression of the 1930s. In Brazil, where inflation rose 1,759 percent in 1989 and approached 5,000 percent by March 1990, business activity came nearly to a standstill while a new government laid off a quarter of its own bloated work force of 1.6 million and sought to remove from circulation some 70 percent of the nation's money supply through freezing interest on savings and various other holdings. For perspective, the U.S. money supply fell by about a third between 1929 and the low point of the Great Depression in 1933.

The United States will probably be spared such Draconian punishment, but something close to it is entirely possible, for the American economy, as this book will document, is far sicker than it should be after so many years of recession-free growth. Oppressive debt permeates all layers of the economy, though the real amount at the federal level is obscured by persistent smoke-and-mirror games in Washington. In global markets, the United States continues to lag behind as a competitor.

Foreign assessments of our situation range from saddened to appalled. For instance, Jacques Attali, a senior aide to French President François Mitterrand, told a recent interviewer that signs of America's decline are "unquestionable." The United States, he added, has become "a nostalgic nation, lacking foresight and turned sadly inward out of resentment over its diminishing weight in the world."[1] His remarks followed such other disheartening examinations of America's prospects as *The Rise and Fall of Great Powers,* an exhaustive study in which Yale historian Paul Kennedy raises the possibility that the United States now faces the sort of decline that overtook such former world powers as Spain and Britain, and *Day of Reckoning,* in which Harvard economist Benjamin Friedman argues that excessive borrowing and anemic saving signal a prolonged erosion of American prosperity and global influence.

There are, to be sure, more hopeful assessments of the U.S. outlook. Writing in *Foreign Affairs,* Samuel P. Huntington, the director of Harvard's Center for International Affairs, maintains that renewal, rather than decline, is in prospect for America. "The United States," he asserts, "is less likely to decline than any other major country," because of "the openness of its economy, society and politics," and he cites "competition, mobility and immigration" as the "engines of renewal." With tongue only partly in cheek, he even finds some merit in the commentary of such analysts as Kennedy and Friedman, inasmuch as "the more Americans worry about the health of their society, the healthier they are."[2]

By mid-1990, there were scattered signs that even the Panglossian administration of George Bush had grown mildly concerned about such matters as the deepening budget deficit. In early May, the president joined with congressional leaders in talks aimed at reining in the deficit through spending cuts and—don't read his lips!—higher taxes. In the workplace, moreover, there was clear evidence of progress. In the automobile industry, there was an unmistakable concern for quality. A survey found that the number of defects per car was down to only 1.5 at Ford, 1.7 at General Motors, and 1.8 at Chrysler. These rates were slightly higher than the Japanese average of 1.2 defects per car. But they were sharply below the comparable rates in 1980 of 6.7 at Ford, 7.4 at GM, and 8.1 at Chrysler. In 1980, the Japanese defect rate had been about two per car, so by 1990 Japan's lead had been greatly narrowed.[3]

But in the main, most problems continued to worsen—from the savings-and-loan debacle to spreading homelessness to a crumbling infrastructure to a deteriorating environment. The prospect of a slumping economy, gripped by the business cycle, can only worsen matters. The situation cries out for bold leadership in the White House and Congress, but there is none. Indeed, officials who speak out too plainly—one such has been L. William Seidman, in charge of bank regulation and helping to manage the S&L bailout—are quietly urged by Bush to accept a comfortable ambassadorship or find employment elsewhere.

As large as the encroaching difficulties may be, so are the opportunities, the foremost of which is the end of the Cold War and the prospect of new markets in Eastern Europe. Even so, to set our house in order we Americans will require far more resolve than we have yet shown, in or out of Washington. The moment is suspenseful: One way or another, the nation will come to live within its means, but will the transformation be a voluntary and orderly endeavor, as this book urges, or will our creditors impose it on us?

WITHIN
OUR
MEANS

CHAPTER ONE

A DAUNTING
NEW DECADE

Historically those people that did not discipline themselves had discipline thrust upon them from the outside. That is why the normal cycle in the life and death of great nations has been first a powerful tyranny broken by revolt, the enjoyment of liberty, the abuse of liberty—and back to tyranny again. As I see it, in this country—a land of the most persistent idealism and the blandest cynicism—the race is on between its decadence and its vitality.
—*Alistair Cooke's America* (1973)

A S A N E W decade dawned in the winter of 1990, the American economy that President Bush had inherited was, despite the surface similarities, vastly changed from the economy of the early Reagan presidency. The presidential rhetoric was upbeat, and Bush stood remarkably high in popularity polls. But even before Iraqi troops rolled through Kuwait ominous developments confronted him that no amount of happy talk and acclaim could alter.

The economy, riding the longest expansion in the nation's peacetime history, was beginning to slow down. Indeed, signs were proliferating that we were on the brink of a new downturn in the business cycle. Yet it was imperative for Bush that activity keep expanding, for with the economy's accumulated imbalances any new recession could prove devastating.

Consider debt. The debt numbers from mid-1981, when the last recession set in, pale when compared to those facing Reagan's successor. As 1990 began, total debt outstanding exceeded 180 percent of the gross national product, a level not seen since the

Great Depression of the 1930s, when the economy was shrinking.

Consumer installment debt was at 16 percent of income, dwarfing all previous readings, and the delinquency rate for consumer loans, at nearly 3 percent, was higher than even in the worst months of the 1981–82 recession.

The volume of business failures, which normally edges down in an expanding economy, was twice as high as when the 1981–82 recession hit bottom and five times higher than at its start.

Meanwhile, the United States had become the world's largest debtor nation, with its investments abroad some $600 billion less than foreigners' U.S. holdings, and debt owed to foreigners, like any other debt, must continue to be serviced in bad times as well as good. Eight years earlier when Reagan took office, the United States had been the world's largest creditor nation.

A worrisome statistic: As the 1990s began, about 90 percent of the total after-tax income of U.S. corporations went to pay the interest on their debt.

This buildup of debt at every level was a ticking time bomb for Bush, set to go off in any major new downturn of the business cycle. To keep the economic expansion rolling after so many years of debt-driven growth was a difficult assignment under any circumstances, and to do so while also trying to discourage still more reckless borrowing—as Bush correctly was attempting to do—was an even greater challenge.

The dilemma for Bush was that the economy's long expansion since November 1982, when the 1981–82 recession finally ended, had been sustained largely through an unprecedented rise in debt in all sectors of the economy. So long as the economy was expanding, this was unlikely to cause widespread debt-servicing problems. However, the history of the business cycle—the economy's long-standing tendency to expand and contract, expand and contract—shows that thick layers of debt invariably have caused severe difficulty once the economy has turned down. In a recession, good debt soon turns into bad debt, and the larger the accumulation beforehand, the longer and deeper the economic slump.

Debt outstanding before the 1981–82 recession, for example, was unusually high and made that slump long and deep, the worst in terms of unemployment, with joblessness reaching 11 percent of the labor force, since the depressed 1930s. When the recession began in mid-1981, overall debt—governmental borrowing as well as private—approximated 140 percent of the gross national product, which was high but still far less than the reading of more than 180 percent that faced Bush in the winter of 1990.

Other debt measures were also relatively high in 1981—such as the amount of consumer installment debt outstanding, at 12 percent of personal income, and the delinquency rate on installment loans, 2.2 percent of which were delinquent thirty days or more. However, the comparable 1990 readings dwarfed these percentages—even though the economy seemed still to be in an expansion phase of the business cycle.

But despite these appearances, there were many signs that overall economic activity was no longer expanding and that we might even be slipping into a new downswing of the business cycle, a new recession. The great rise in debt also appeared, by no coincidence, to be ending. Overall borrowing continued to rise, to be sure, but the annual rate of climb had slowed to only about 4 percent, down from rates of more than 14 percent in some of the Reagan years.

In one sense, this slowing was welcome news, for the surge in debt in the 1980s was widely seen as unsustainable and ultimately dangerous to the economy's long-term health. A lighter debt load in the new decade portended less inflation and lower interest rates.

But there was a catch. Because the economy had been running on credit for so long, the debt slowdown also foreshadowed a sluggish business pace, and perhaps even a recession which, with the continuing burden of past borrowing, could prove severe indeed.

The borrowing binge of the 1980s had been enormous. In 1988, total debt outstanding reached a peak of 186 percent of the gross national product, against an average of slightly less than 140 percent through most of the post–World War II era. But by 1990, the debt level had eased to 182 percent of the gross national product, after a slower increase in total debt outstanding in 1989 than in any year since 1975, a time of deep recession.

Behind this new slowdown in borrowing was the fact that much of the debt created in the 1980s simply could no longer be serviced. Since it could not be financed out of current income streams, it was being written off. This, typically, is what happens after any long borrowing binge. When loans turn sour, a lender's first step usually is to increase loan-loss reserves. Sooner or later some of the worst loans are written off, and when this happens, debt outstanding falls.

This was the case, for example, when just before Christmas 1989 Bankers Trust New York Corp. announced a $90 million after-tax charge against earnings for two bad loans. A short while earlier, Bank of New England, with many troubled real-estate loans, announced plans to write off about $175 million of loans in the last quarter of 1989. Such moves tend, of course, to cut overall debt. Even so, business debt outstanding still topped $2 trillion as 1990 began.

Even larger was the consumer debt load of $4.3 trillion, and, like businesses, consumers were beginning to try to cut their debts. A new mood of caution was emerging. In a University of Michigan survey, the consumers expressing a willingness to borrow fell from 35 percent in mid-1986 to 19 percent.

People seemed ever so gingerly to be edging back to the more conservative behavior of the 1950s, when memories of the Great Depression were still in mind. Moreover, the Tax Reform Act of 1986 had progressively curbed deductions for interest payments. Interest on personal loans was limited in 1990 to 10 percent of the interest incurred, down from a 1989 limit of 20 percent, and plans called for no interest deductibility on such loans in 1991.

This more cautious mood was evident in a tendency to save more income. During the 1980s, savings amounted to less than 3 percent of after-tax income in some months, but in 1990 the rate was above 5 percent, and many economists predicted it would reach 8 percent or 10 percent in the next few years.

Federal debt, which had grown to more than $3 trillion in 1990, was also mounting more slowly. Behind this slowing was a gradual shrinkage in the budget deficit, as officially reported. Though still huge, the official federal budget deficit had narrowed appreciably since mid-1986, when it reached a record annual rate of about $240 billion. More recently, the official rate had slipped below $150 billion, and further declines were forecast—incorrectly, as things developed—by officials of the Bush administration.

The Gramm-Rudman-Hollings Act, requiring automatic spending cuts each year, had lent a modicum of discipline to budget policy, though rules allowing the inclusion of mounting Social Security surpluses in budget calculations made the balances seem deceptively healthy.

T H E job that George Bush inherited from Ronald Reagan on January 20, 1989, might seem in some respects enviable. For all the burdens of presidential office, the nation on that date was at peace, with its economy rolling through a seventh year of uninterrupted expansion. Inflation and unemployment were far lower than early in the decade, and corporate profits and the stock market, even after the October 1987 crash, were higher.

Still, staggering numbers are needed to describe the bills confronting Bush as he took office. Costs for Medicare and Medicaid were rising at a pace that dwarfed the overall rise of Social Security. The bill for the health programs was set to jump nearly 13 percent in 1990, to $148 billion, against a relatively modest rise of about 4 percent for Social Security as a whole. As medical science progressed against such killers as cardiovascular disease, more of the population were dying from such relatively expensive-to-treat diseases as cancer. People were living longer.

Litigiousness, with its inevitable impact on medical insurance charges, also drove up the health-care bill. And, of course, there was the increasing expense of modern, high-technology medicine, able to diagnose and treat once-untreatable illnesses. Some 37 million Americans, moreover, were without any health insurance at all as Bush's presidency began, and about two-thirds of these people worked full-time or were dependents, mainly children, of full-time workers. When Reagan became president, only about 25 million Americans had no insurance.

There was also, of course, the mounting bill for AIDS. In 1988, the Department of Health and Human Services had projected that within three years the annual bill for AIDS patients would approach $5 billion, but only a year later this figure was revised up to nearly $9 billion. Treating a single AIDS patient in 1988 cost, on the average, $57,000, and there were some 73,000 of them. Looking ahead, the patient total was expected to quadruple in four years.

In all, Americans were spending about $600 billion a year in private and public funds on health care when Bush came to the White House. This amounted to some 12 percent of the gross national product, a far higher rate than in such other nations as France (8 percent), Canada (8 percent), West Germany (8 percent), Japan (7 percent), and Britain (6 percent). And the U.S. tab was escalating at an annual rate of nearly 9 percent a year, more than twice the pace of inflation. Without a greater effort to curb this spiral, the health-care bill by the late 1990s would reach about $1.5 trillion, a daunting number.

Another soaring expense was the drug problem. Seemingly insolvable, it was linked not only to the nation's high crime rate but to the huge, mounting health-care bill. A congressional study found in 1989 that, largely because of drugs, emergency-room cases were soaring in most large-city hospitals. In New Orleans, the number of emergency-room admissions rose 210 percent, in Philadelphia 199 percent, and in Washington 134 percent. Around the same time, General Motors Corp. detailed how drug abuse can affect a major company. It cost GM more than $1 billion a year in worker absenteeism and addiction treatment efforts that often reached $20,000 a year per patient. GM estimated that the typical drug abuser in its work force was on the job only 140 days a year.

No less challenging than health care for the new administration, but of longer-range concern, was industrial pollution. The problem's roots extended back beyond the Reagan presidency, but as George M. Woodwell, director of the Woods Hole Research Center in Massachusetts, observed, in "the Reagan era, eight years of subsidized avarice [put] the cap on a monument of flaws in the management of growth and in the stewardship of resources."[1]

The problem for Bush was many-sided. It was increasingly clear that industrial-waste gases such as chlorofluorocarbons, methane, and carbon dioxide were causing a slow warming of the atmosphere—the so-called greenhouse effect—which threatened, for instance, to raise the sea level some three feet over the course of the next century. Merely to protect U.S. coastal cities from such a sea-level rise could cost $111 billion, according to the Environmental Protection Agency, and without a major shift to cleaner energy sources the full cost of the greenhouse effect over the next century was put at $3.6 trillion. Two economists, Alan S. Manne of Stanford University and Richard G. Richels of the Electric Power Research Institute, estimated that even with such an energy shift the cleanup would cost a still-awesome $800 billion.

Americans were generating some twenty-five tons of waste annually per capita, only 3 percent of which was actually household garbage. The bulk was from sewage, factories, and agriculture, which accounted for 65 percent of the pollutants entering American streams and rivers. When Bush became president, more than $300 billion already had been spent under the Clean Water Act of 1972 to control water pollution, and partly as a result, the number of Americans served by sewage-treatment plants rose to 127 million from 85 million. Yet the 1972 act was at best a holding action marked as much by its inadequacies as by its successes, and a far stronger commitment was sorely needed. But the construction cost of a single incinerator was as high as $500 million. As many as 155 such plants were in use and twenty-nine were under construction when Bush took office, but another sixty-four had been delayed or canceled because of climbing costs.

Problems also plagued the Environmental Protection Agency's much-publicized Superfund program. Financed through taxes on industries generating toxic waste, the Superfund was enacted in 1980 to rid the nation of hazardous dumps, but by 1989 it had spent as much as $4 billion to clean up only forty-three dumps, while an estimated ten thousand others awaited action. The cleanup cost of a single site ran as high as $300 million, and the wait between the time a dump was targeted for cleanup and the start of work was nearly nine years. A huge added expense was the cleanup of the dangerous mess created by more than a dozen nuclear-weapons facilities, some more than forty years old, where safety procedures had grown woefully lax. The Energy Department placed this bill, plus the cost of needed renovations at some of the aging facilities, at about $200 billion.

Another enormous expense was the inevitable result of a demographic trend. There were 3.3 workers for each Social Security recipient in 1989, but this ratio, which had been as high as 5.1 in the early 1960s, would drop as the average age of the work force, as well as of the population generally, rose. When the big post–World War II contingent of baby boomers would be retiring within two decades or so, the ratio would drop to only 2.4, and a further decline to 1.9 would soon follow. At some $50 billion when Bush took office, the surplus in the Social Security Trust Fund was projected to keep rising until the baby-boom retirement wave, and the eventual surplus in theory would reach a colossal $12 trillion, more than enough to finance the anticipated retirements. But the surplus was being spent, not saved, and so a challenge for Bush was to stop this deception. It was little comfort that, based on expected modest inflation over the next couple of decades, the sum needed, in terms of the dollar's 1988 buying power, would be only $2.35 trillion.

T H E bailout of the savings-and-loan industry also entailed huge costs. But there was a subtler and in some respects more difficult challenge. The bailout law—formally titled the Financial Institutions Reform, Recovery and Enforcement Act of 1989, or FIRREA—was crucial to bringing the thrift crisis under control and establishing rules to supervise and finance the rescue operation. But it left a critical matter unsettled, since it allowed deposits to be insured by the federal government as before, for up to $100,000. This guarantee had contributed greatly to the S&L mess in the first place. With the irresponsible deregulation of the Reagan era, many S&Ls had plowed money into all sorts of new, questionable deals and yet enjoyed deposit protection. With no change in this insurance arrangement, FIRREA could not really curb risk-taking sufficiently. Its new regulatory machinery, while an improvement over the setup under Reagan, still was not extensive enough to oversee the thousands of thrift units still operating. With deposit insurance reduced or eliminated, instead of allowed to continue, depositors would be warier about placing funds in high-yielding thrifts. Market forces in the end would provide an additional degree of policing impossible through FIRREA.

But how should such a step be implemented? And if the government were to insure deposits only partly or not at all, might not the risk of a 1930s-style credit collapse outweigh any possible gains? Federal deposit insurance was introduced in the 1930s precisely to prevent a repetition of the banking failures that deepened the Great Depression. So the challenge for Bush went far beyond FIRREA and the amount of bailout money needed.

A more pressing S&L matter was to sell off assets of failed units. FIRREA regulators were assigned to liquidate more than $100 billion worth of office buildings, raw land, shopping centers, and housing, and the task was not made easier by rules tending to protect a politically powerful, jittery real-estate industry. The regulators needed at least two appraisals for each property to be sold, and in no case were they to sell any real estate at less than 95 percent of its appraised value. Several months after the selling effort was launched, daily sales were averaging only $2.8 million, an impossibly slow pace suggesting it would take some 140 years to dispose of all the property.

While the S&L crisis grabbed major headlines in Bush's early months, a crisis of another sort was slowly building at state and local governments. The much-publicized tax-cutting of the Reagan years had shifted much of the fiscal burden at the federal level to the states and localities. As a result, the financial health of these governments was deteriorating sharply as Bush took office. State governments had registered a surplus of $800 million in their combined operating budgets in 1985, but Reagan's final years were marked by deepening state deficits—$600 million in 1986, more than $9 billion in 1987, and $16.5 billion in 1988—and the situation was continuing to worsen under Bush. The pattern was evident, for example, in Connecticut, once fiscally sound, whose officials predicted in late November that the state would probably run up a deficit in fiscal 1990 of $51.5 million because of rapidly rising expenses and disappointing revenues. Only a month earlier, Connecticut officials had forecast a $2.6 million surplus for the year. This darkening fiscal outlook occurred even though the state had recently enacted nearly $1 billion in tax increases, including a boost in its sales tax to 8 percent from 7.5 percent. Serving to drive up spending, meanwhile, were such state needs as an additional $4.6 million for day-care programs,

$3.5 million for prison dormitories, and $1.6 million for mental-health facilities.

At local-government level, the picture was much the same. Localities, ranging from large cities to towns and school districts, showed a combined surplus of $13 billion in 1985, a smaller surplus of $6.2 billion in 1986, and then deepening deficits of $3.1 billion in 1987 and $4.9 billion in 1988. Between 1985 and 1988, by no coincidence, federal grants to these localities fell from $19.1 billion to $14.5 billion. Yet these governments carried the main responsibility for financing the most pressing public needs, such as police and fire protection, sanitation, road repair, and education. For Los Angeles to have provided simply average-quality services for its residents in 1989, the city would have had to raise its revenues 80 percent, and New York City would have needed a 63 percent increase.[2] Even without such increases, the two cities, as well as others like them, were having to raise taxes repeatedly, and this was prompting businesses and families to move out, which of course brought a further decline in the cities' fiscal health. This vicious circle posed a challenge for the Bush team that could be met only if the federal government, which had turned its back on state and local needs and was itself deeply in debt, adopted new policies. The federal government needed to shift more of its limited resources from outdated Cold War arms programs to states and localities fighting an assortment of domestic ills, from homelessness to a crumbling infrastructure.

Elementary and secondary education has long been the major expense for local governments. When Bush took office, some 27 million adult Americans were functionally illiterate, without the minimal reading, writing, or math skills needed to hold a job, and another 72 million lacked the capacity to find work for themselves or to meet changing job requirements.[3] Nor was the outlook for younger Americans promising. In early 1989, a National Science Foundation study found that American thirteen-year-olds scored at the bottom in an international comparison of math and science skills. South Korean thirteen-year-olds scored four times higher than the average for U.S. youths in math and nearly twice the U.S. average in science. Other nations in the study included Britain, Ireland, Spain, and Canada. Bassan Z. Shakhahirir, an assistant director at NSF, remarked that "the lack of preparation for further education and future employment that these American teen-agers demonstrated is nothing short of frightening." Bush came to the White House promising to be "the education president," but his budget contained less for education than Reagan's last one. Clearly, a major new effort would be necessary for Bush to fulfill that promise.

To make America at least a fairer nation, if not necessarily gentler and kinder, the Bush administration would have to seek still firmer federal control over a range of problems, from pollution to the investment activities of thrift institutions to the trading practices of self-regulatory securities exchanges. Some effort toward reregulation had begun, to be sure, but much work remained, for the quality of the federal establishment had deteriorated seriously under Reagan. Soon after Bush took office, a presidential commission concluded that federal employees were badly underpaid, compared to their civilian counterparts. The gap was 28.6 percent, on the average, and to close it would cost about $35 billion. Under Reagan, federal wage increases ranged from none at all in some years to a high of 4.8 percent, which still was not enough to offset inflation. Not surprisingly, morale in most federal agencies was low. At the Social Security Administration, for instance, 51 percent of the agency's personnel had "poor or extremely poor" morale, up from 43 percent two years earlier, and 74 percent of the employees felt overworked. In the preceding six years, by no coincidence, the agency sustained a 20 percent cut in the size of its work force.[4]

T H E United States, meanwhile, had become increasingly beholden to foreigners, a result of the massive foreign trade deficits under Reagan, which transformed America from the world's largest creditor nation into the world's largest debtor. Americans now owed foreigners some $600 billion more than foreigners owed the United States. In 1987, Japan surpassed the United States, in dollar terms, as the world's richest nation in overall wealth as well as on a per capita basis. The total dollar value of Japan's assets—its land, factories, stocks, and other wealth—reached $43.7 trillion, up from $28.3 trillion in 1986 and $19.6 trillion in 1985. Similarly measured, U.S. wealth in 1987 totaled

$36.2 trillion, up from $34 trillion in 1986 and $30.6 trillion in 1985. Thus, Japan's wealth in the three years rose from $11 trillion less than ours to $7.5 trillion more.

A more subtle, more troubling reflection of America's diminished world stature shows up in little-publicized financial data which reflect the appraisals of investors. When Reagan took office, the New York Stock Exchange accounted for some 55 percent of the combined value of all the world's stock markets, and when he left this share had fallen to slightly under 30 percent. Meanwhile, in the same eight years, the Tokyo stock market's share of global equity expanded to 47 percent from only 17 percent.[5]

For all of this, the dollar remained the world's premier currency throughout the Reagan presidency. But this reflected considerations far removed from the financial arena. America remained a military superpower, capable of obliterating any attacker, and so the dollar, in effect backed by thousands of thermonuclear bombs residing in missile silos and on submarines, held an attraction not offered by, say, the Japanese yen or the West German mark. It provided the ultimate capital haven for the long haul in a nuclear-armed world. And because other nations still were willing to hold dollars as a monetary reserve in their central-bank coffers, the United States retained privileges not available to nations with currencies of lesser rank; the dollar's reserve-currency status allowed the United States to continue merrily along a path of woefully unbalanced foreign trade, buying far more in goods and services from abroad than it sold there.

Even so, America's cherished ability, as a superpower, to be the master of its economic fate, to be self-reliant, was greatly reduced by 1990. The independence of the Federal Reserve Board diminished sharply, for the central bank no longer was able to set interest rates and regulate the quantity of money available with little or no regard for how its moves might play abroad. A change in interest rates, intended to spur or slow business activity at home, might be abandoned purely for international considerations, such as how a particular action might affect Japanese investment flows into the United States. The new, overriding concern in Washington was how any such policy moves might be received by investors in Tokyo and Frankfurt, whose willingness to hold huge quantities of dollars was necessary to finance our massive budget deficits.

At a Treasury auction in the latter part of 1988, the Japanese snapped up half of all ten-year and thirty-year securities offered by the U.S. agency. Without such support from foreign buyers, the Treasury's enormous financing requirements would have weighed far more heavily on U.S. credit markets, driving up interest rates and diverting investment funds from more productive avenues within the economy's private sector.

This concern at the Fed about reaction abroad to its policy shifts was something new. The independence of U.S. monetary authorities had once been the envy of central bankers elsewhere. But no longer. Late in Reagan's presidency, foreign holdings of U.S. debt—federal plus corporate and consumer—came to nearly 10 percent of all debt outstanding in the nation. When Reagan took office the rate was only 4 percent.

The most disquieting fact was that the Fed had lost much of its power to combat an incipient economic slump—typically through lowering interest rates and pumping up the money supply. Henry Kaufman, an economic adviser to the Fed, warned that in the event of a recession any "unilateral" lowering of interest rates by the Fed to revive the domestic economy could well prompt foreigners to "stampede" away from Treasury securities, which in turn "would force interest rates even higher and thus worsen the recession."[6]

Washington's other traditional weapon against a recession is deficit spending. But Reagan's deficits raised a question about how much deeper into deficit the budget could reasonably be put, even in the event of a recession. The accompanying cartoon, which appeared in the last year of Reagan's presidency, shows the predicament facing Bush as the 1990s began.

Events surrounding the stock market crash of October 1987 also help illustrate the new climate in which the Fed was forced to operate. Before the market's plunge, foreign investors had grown increasingly uneasy about U.S. economic policy, with the persistent, massive budget and trade deficits and the apparent disregard in the White House for the dollar's diminishing international worth. Jittery over the prospect of clinging to large invest-

ments denominated in a depreciating currency, many foreigners began to dump dollar holdings and shied away from new commitments. Many Americans did the same. The impact—despite the Fed's relatively easy monetary stance at the time—was to drive up rates of fixed-income securities denominated in dollars, such as Treasury bonds. This, in turn, helped set the stage for the sharpest one-day drop in the market's history up to that time—the 508-point plunge in the Dow Jones Industrial Average on October 19, 1987.

As Bush took office in early 1989, there was gathering concern among U.S. policymakers, remembering October 1987, over how foreign investors viewed the U.S. economy. The Atlanta Federal Reserve Bank warned that "foreigners are losing patience with American inaction on the federal budget." The bank went on to caution that foreigners "may pull back their participation in the government bond market should the new administration fail to make real and quick progress on the deficit."[7] About the same time, *The Wall Street Journal* cited "foreign pressure" on the Bush administration to cut the deficit, which was running at an annual rate of about $160 billion. The White House was said to be fuming at this foreign interference, but was nonetheless responding with a greater effort to comply.[8]

By the time Bush was in the White House, some analysts on Wall Street had become almost nostalgic. "Not long ago, the Federal Reserve was arbiter of money and credit in the domestic economy; to determine if the United States was liquid or not, one had only to track the creation of reserve bank credit through the U.S. commercial banking system," recalled James Grant in his financial newsletter. But now, he added with resignation, "the Fed is gradually losing control of policy."[9] Going further, David Hale of the Kemper Group noted the "remarkable patience" of the Japanese with a spendthrift America and added, "The buoyant economic backdrop to the Bush inauguration is far more of a tribute to Japanese economic policy and financial power than it is a celebration of American economic policy."[10] By agreeing to help prop up the dollar, Japan was allowing the American expansion to go on.

Growing foreign power within the U.S. financial community was widespread. When Reagan left office, 260 foreign banks operated in the United States, and they controlled 21 percent of the nation's domestic banking operations, up from 14 percent six years earlier. In California alone, the most populous state, Japanese banks held about 25 percent of the market. Greenwich Associates, a Connecticut consultant, estimated that 45 percent of all large U.S. corporations used at least one Japanese bank. Other studies found that Japanese banks were run more efficiently and therefore were able to lend more cheaply. First Manhattan Consulting Group estimated that a typical American bank needed to price its loans about 2 percentage points over cost to make a sufficient profit, against a spread of only one percentage point for a Japanese bank.

When the stock market crashed in 1987, the Federal Reserve quickly ordered several large New York banks to make funds readily available to any securities firms threatening to fail as a result of stock plunge, and several were indeed kept afloat by the fast cooperation of these banks. However, the rescue operation would not have been so swift, and far deeper financial damage could have occurred, had the Fed been compelled to deal with banks headquartered in, say, Tokyo or London rather than in New York.

A M E R I C A ' S waning economic independence in the Reagan years was most glaringly evident, perhaps, in the shrinking share of things sold in the U.S. marketplace that were actually made in America. Many imported items, it should be added, had been pioneered in the United States, including color television sets, audio tape recorders, videocassette recorders, ball bearings, telephone receivers, and phonographs. Yet in the Reagan presidency the shares of such items supplied to U.S. customers by U.S. manufacturers narrowed sharply, Commerce Department data show. The share for color TV sets fell from 60 percent to less than 10 percent; for audio and video recorders from roughly 10 percent to zero; for ball bearings from about 75 percent to 70 percent; for telephone receivers from 90 percent to less than 20 percent; and for phonographs from 30 percent to zero. Such shrinkage occurred even though, for all the White House rhetoric about the virtues of free trade, the share of U.S. imports subject to some form of restraint rose to 24 percent from 12 percent.

This diminished self-reliance was evident in an area America once dominated—the most advanced technologies. When Reagan left the White House, U.S. manufacturers had virtually abandoned trying to compete with Japanese producers in the development, for instance, of a whole new generation of computer devices—4-megabit memory chips, so called because they can each store up to four million pieces of information. Production lines for these chips were springing up on Kyushu, the island that is Japan's highly sophisticated version of California's Silicon Valley, and the cost of these lines, as high as $400 million each, was simply out of reach for would-be American competitors.

Another high-tech area where U.S. firms had become virtual nonparticipants was high-definition television transmission, which among other advantages provides far crisper TV images. Sensing its importance, the Commerce Department and the American Electronics Association moved in January 1989 to encourage such premier U.S. firms as International Business Machines, American Telephone & Telegraph, Digital Equipment, Hewlett-Packard, Zenith, Texas Instruments, and Motorola to form a partnership to develop a U.S. high-definition TV industry in the United States. However, as Steven Jobs, the founder of Apple Computer, put it bluntly, "All this stuff about how the U.S. is going to participate is a joke," for the U.S. could no longer compete even in the production of regular television transmission.[11] This growing inability to compete in so many manufacturing fields in the Reagan years also cost the nation millions of relatively highly paid, skilled jobs. In 1987, this loss amounted to 5.1 million mostly well-paid jobs.

In 1988, the top three firms in worldwide sales of manufacturing material for semiconductor companies were foreign-owned: Nikon, with sales of $520 million; Tokyo Electron, with sales of $510 million; and Advantest, with sales of $385 million. A decade earlier, the top six were all U.S. companies. This little-known industry produces silicon wafers, etching equipment, and other items essential in the manufacture of computer chips, and its slippage in America in the Reagan years helps explain the sharp decline of the entire U.S. semiconductor industry. Before Bush had been in office ten months, the largest of the remaining U.S. producers of chip-making equipment, Perkin-Elmer Corp., was negotiating with Nikon to sell the Japanese company its chip-making operation. Only a decade earlier, Perkin-Elmer had pioneered the development of chip production. The deal eventually fell through, partly because Nikon's interest in the acquisition declined.

More and more U.S. jobs, meanwhile, were in the service of foreign owners. By the end of Reagan's tenure, 35 percent of the American chemical industry was foreign-owned. In 1988 alone, 203 U.S. concerns were acquired by the Japanese, up from 146 such takeovers in 1987. This brought the number of Japanese-owned, U.S.-based manufacturing concerns to 890.

U.S. businesses bought by foreigners in 1988 included Macmillan Publishing, taken over by Britain's Maxwell Communication;

Triangle Publications, the issuer of *TV Guide* and *Seventeen* magazine, by News Corp. of Australia; Telex, the producer of communications terminals, by Memorex International of the Netherlands; Staley Continental, the food-service and corn-products firm, by Britain's Tate & Lyle; Firestone Tire & Rubber, by Bridgestone of Japan; Tropicana Products, by Seagram of Canada; G. Heileman Brewing, the maker of Old Style and Colt 45, by Australia's Bond Corp. Holdings; and CBS Records, by Japan's Sony.

The takeovers also involved large amounts of U.S. real estate. By 1988, the Japanese owned more than a third of downtown Los Angeles and part or full interests in such prestigious office towers as the Exxon Building and Park Avenue Plaza in New York City, Citicorp Center in San Francisco, and ARCO Plaza in Los Angeles—the purchases of New York's Rockefeller Center and California's magnificent Pebble Beach golf course were still to come.

American managers working for Japanese-owned firms in the United States were discovering, meanwhile, that their opportunities to advance within such organizations often were limited. A study of thirty-one such companies by the University of Michigan concluded that "Japanese firms are great places to begin or end careers, but they are not places where Americans see opportunities for long-term career progression." Among Americans who quit high-level jobs with Japanese-run firms in this period were the two top U.S. managers at Mazda Motor Corp.'s Flat Rock, Michigan, assembly plant. They were replaced by Japanese executives.

In December 1988, a team of Yale economists estimated that within a couple of decades, with present trends, Japan and West Germany together would own about 35 percent of all American industry. Unless "trends change drastically," the report warned, the United States would find itself "heavily indebted" to supplying huge dividend and interest payments to foreign proprietors, with less profits available for use at home. Without a change, there would be a twentyfold increase in the next decade in the amount of U.S. industry owned, for example, by Japan and West Germany, in which case America's dividend and interest payments to those two countries alone could reach $65 billion. And this assumes that interest rates remain low.

Benjamin M. Friedman, the Harvard economist, warned, "We are surrendering the ownership of our country's productive assets, not in exchange for assets we will own abroad but merely to finance our overconsumption," in sorry contrast to "our traditional self-perception of America as a nation of owners."[12] Albert M. Wojnilower of First Boston Corp. forecast in September 1988 that it would become increasingly difficult for Americans to maintain their living standards because of their growing need "ultimately to work for others to pay for our trade deficit." In Tokyo, Kenichi Ohmae, the manager of McKinsey & Co.'s office there, warned that "America's most competitive 'exports' today are land, houses, and companies." America was selling itself to foreigners—and with a cheap dollar.

Some admirers of Reagan's economic policies, such as Milton Friedman, the economist at the Hoover Institution, contend that this surge in foreign investment was a blessing in that it created countless new jobs for Americans, as well as highly efficient new factories, such as the automobile plants built by Honda, Toyota, and Nissan. However, most foreign investment was for existing facilities and therefore contributed barely 1 percent of all new jobs generated in the United States between 1984 and 1986. Much of it also reflected a desire to hedge against the possibility of increased U.S. protectionism. By early 1990, Japanese-owned "transplants" accounted for nearly a quarter of the cars being produced in the United States, an increase of more than 50 percent in only a year.

These takeovers intensified foreign lobbying in Washington. Foreign corporations managed to kill a bill in 1988 requiring more detailed reporting of investment from abroad. Foreign corporations set up political action committees and hired such figures as Walter Mondale and Elliot Richardson. In January 1989, Touche Ross & Co., the accounting firm, queried hundreds of top U.S. executives about the impact of foreign investment and found that 71 percent favored some degree of restriction on foreign ownership of "industries essential to our national interest." One in five also felt that the investment inflow threatened even America's "social and cultural foundations."

. . .

T H E least-noticed area of foreign dependency for the United States when Reagan left office was, ironically, where he had directed the most attention: the military establishment. It was increasingly dependent on foreigners. In 1987, British Aerospace bought a stake of more than 40 percent in Reflectone Inc., a Florida maker of flight simulators and information systems for the military. A short while later, Britain's Plessy PLC purchased Sippican Inc., a Massachusetts manufacturer of oceanic research instruments for the Navy. The U.S. government had the power to block such takeovers, but rarely exercised it.

A jarring sign of America's reduced self-reliance in defense involved another Japanese company, Toshiba Corp., which had provided the expertise, through its machine-tool operations, for the design of the super-secret propellers on certain U.S. nuclear submarines. It came to light that Toshiba had also provided the Russians with this expertise, which U.S. authorities claimed had compromised the Navy's submarine force. The United States imposed penalties against Toshiba, but the larger point was that America's machine-tool industry had grown so feeble that it could not engineer a highly secret component crucial to the U.S. military.

In early 1989, the Pentagon warned Congress that "in key niches of microelectronics, optics, superconductivity and information-systems technologies, Japan either holds or shares a worldwide lead" and urged increased "cooperative arms developments" between the United States and Japan. One such effort was an agreement in November 1988 to build jointly an FSX-type fighter plane. But Japan's Mitsubishi Heavy Industries already had developed an FSX equipped with Russian engines that, while somewhat slower than similar U.S. models, could make a 360-degree turn in only one-third as much airspace, a crucial advantage. The Japanese plane also had superior ceramic and carbon-fiber technology. Altogether, the venture was more a chance for the United States to benefit from Japanese know-how than the other way around.

A disquieting assessment of America's defense capacity as Bush arrived in the White House came from Shintaro Ishihara, a leading Japanese politician and an advocate of a very hard line in his country's dealings with Washington. No matter how much

Americans beef up their military, he told a Tokyo audience, "they have come to the point that they could do nothing if Japan were one day to say, 'We will no longer sell you chips.' " He overstated the situation, but perhaps not too greatly, when he added, "Should Japan decide to sell its chips to the Soviet Union instead, that would instantly alter the balance of power."

The most disheartening sign of America's reliance on foreign expertise was how foreign science had come to dominate the American scientific scene. In 1987, the three companies granted the most patents in the United States were all Japanese—Canon, with 847 patents; Hitachi, with 845; and Toshiba, with 823. In 1982, General Electric led the patent parade with 739, and only one Japanese firm, Hitachi, was among the top three. In all, foreign inventors captured 47 percent of patents granted in the United States in 1987, up from 35 percent a decade earlier. Particularly striking was America's slippage in the pharmaceutical field, where it had long excelled. Between 1976 and 1980, U.S. companies introduced seventy new drugs, double the number originating from Japan. But in the last five years of Reagan's presidency, Japanese firms introduced sixty new drugs, against fifty-eight for U.S. manufacturers.

Just after Bush's inauguration, Texas Senator Lloyd Bentsen told an audience of top U.S. business executives of his wife's reaction to the news that he had agreed to speak before a powerful, prestigious group that evening. She remarked, Bentsen said with a straight face, "Oh, so you're going to Tokyo."

CHAPTER TWO

A FADING DREAM

No democracy has been less interested in its failures; in an economic sense, no democracy has so magnificently rewarded its successful men or been so continuously convinced that prosperity was always round the corner.
—Harold J. Laski, *The American Democracy* (1948)

B Y T H E T I M E George Bush entered the White House, there were signs that the dream that each new generation of Americans would enjoy a higher standard of living was beginning to fade.

This became apparent to me, for example, during my occasional visits as a guest journalist to various college campuses. I recall, particularly, several days that I spent late in Reagan's presidency in Cambridge, Massachusetts, interviewing seniors at Harvard. I was preparing a report for *The Wall Street Journal* on what seemed puzzling: At Harvard as well as at many other colleges, economics, which was once far down the list of favorite courses, had recently become by a wide margin the most popular major, or area of concentration, to use Harvard's particular terminology.

I soon discovered that this newfound popularity of a subject deemed deadly dull by most undergraduates in my ancient college days at Yale had nothing whatever to do with any new interest in economic theories. Rather, an economics major was widely seen as the fastest, surest route to a high-paying job on Wall Street, where fortunes were indeed being made by men and women not much older than those I was interviewing in Cambridge. A Harvard senior from an upper-middle-class background in the Midwest told me he was trying to decide whether to accept a high-paying job offer from Morgan Stanley or from Goldman, Sachs, both eminent investment banking insitutions, and he added: "I didn't study economics because I'm fascinated by the distinctions between the concepts of John Maynard Keynes and Milton Friedman, but because I want to make enough money to live at least as well as my parents, and that is getting harder and harder to do."

Studies support this view. A survey by *The Wall Street Journal* and NBC News in early 1989 found that, despite "seven years of solid economic growth, Americans who think the standard of living is falling narrowly outnumber those who think it is rising." The poll further found that 63 percent of the population felt their generation was "better off" than that of their parents, but only 40 percent were confident that their children's generation would be so fortunate.

The gist of a 250-page study by a team of economists at the Brookings Institution in Washington was that "American living standards have been sheltered" from a sharp decline through borrowing, particularly through borrowing from foreigners. However, the report warned "that the situation is unraveling" and hard times will confront the new Bush presidency, though they hadn't yet arrived with the start of the new decade in the winter of 1990.[1]

Evidence that such an unraveling was already under way in 1988 was buried in data from Washington's busy number mills— not in such headline-grabbing statistics as the gross national product or the consumer price index or the unemployment rate, but in such relatively obscure series as the inflation-adjusted level of weekly and hourly earnings. At election time in 1988, the average weekly earnings of workers in the economy's nonfarm private sector stood at $326.87, nearly $12 higher than in 1981, Reagan's first year.

That may seem a respectable increase—until one takes inflation into account. To do this, the government produces a second weekly-pay series, relatively unpublicized, that expresses pay in terms of the dollar's buying power in a particular year, 1977. By this measure, weekly earnings in November 1988 averaged only $167.45, down $2.68 from the comparable 1981 level. The buying power of the average American worker actually fell over the course of the Reagan presidency. And if one goes back to 1980, a recession year, the loss of buying power works out to $5.29 a week. Buying power peaked as long ago as 1972—at $198.41, in terms of the 1977 dollar. This, of course, was before the economy was ravaged by repeated bouts of high inflation, Arab oil squeezes, and several severe recessions in which the jobless rate was as high as 11 percent of the labor force.

Other government data show that hourly pay levels also rose briskly during the Reagan years, but only if inflation isn't considered. The hourly rate in November 1988 was one-third greater than in 1981. But when an adjustment is made for inflation, this gain evaporates. Like the weekly pay figure, inflation-adjusted hourly pay had been edging down since early in the previous decade.

S O why were so many Americans still so sanguine about their circumstances under Reagan? On Christmas morning 1988, the final Christmas of the long Reagan presidency, newspapers across the United States carried the results of a new Gallup Poll. Among the findings was that 56 percent of those surveyed—1,001 adult Americans from New York to California—were satisfied "with the way things are going" in the nation. This was a sharply higher satisfaction rate than only a year before, when 45 percent of the respondents expressed such a view. The Christmas 1988 poll found, moreover, that 87 percent of those interviewed were also satisfied "with the way things are going" in their personal lives. Up from 84 percent at Christmastime in 1987, this marked the highest personal-satisfaction reading in the poll's ten-year history.

The sense of satisfaction found by the Gallup Poll near the finish of Reagan's presidency reflected various facts. In December 1988, American business was rolling through the seventy-third consecutive month of an economic expansion that had begun all the way back in November 1982. It was by far the longest expansion in the nation's peacetime experience, surpassed only by a 106-month-long upturn in the 1960s, during the Vietnam War. It was an expansion, moreover, that most business forecasters had initially presumed would be, if not stillborn, exceedingly short-lived, for it developed under circumstances that hardly seemed conducive to prolonged business growth.

In the conventional economic wisdom of the time, it seemed downright ominous that the average interest rate carried on highly rated corporate bonds was close to 12 percent, or that new-home mortgage rates were averaging near 14 percent, or that commercial banks were charging in the neighborhood of 12 percent on their loans to prime customers. These were not, surely, the economic circumstances in which sustained recoveries of business activity developed. Nor was it heartening, in November 1982, that consumer prices, on the average, were some 6 percent higher than a year before. This rate of climb, were it to persist, would approximately halve the dollar's buying power in roughly eight years.

For all of this, more than six years later, in the closing days of the Reagan presidency, the economy remained on the same expansionary path that first developed when interest rates and inflation were so high and most forecasters so pessimistic.

There were many remarkable reflections of the economy's continuing vigor at the end of the Reagan years. There was, for instance, a December 1988 survey of the membership of the National Association of Purchasing Management, the trade association for thousands of corporate buying agents around the country. The report, issued on January 3, 1989, only days before Reagan was to depart for his beloved California, stated that the economy had closed 1988 "with vigorous growth." Indeed, it declared that "December exited like a lion." And all the while, it added, inflation appeared to be—*mirabile dictu!*—in "a solid downtrend." There were few signs, the survey concluded, of any "slowing in this, the seventh year, of the recovery."

Around the same time, the Commerce Department's annual estimate of the outlook for U.S. industry in the year ahead flashed a reassuring message. Assessing 1989 prospects in more than 350 businesses in both the goods-producing and the service-providing sectors, the Commerce Department report concluded that general growth would persist through the new year, at the least, with producers of electronic and high-technology goods leading the parade, to be followed closely by capital-equipment manufacturers. Vigor was apparent, among other places, in the estimate that shipments of metal-cutting machines—a long-standing barometer of how business planners regard their companies' prospects—would surge as much as 13.9 percent, after taking inflation into account.

As Reagan prepared to head for California, the nation's so-called misery index—which economists calculate by simply adding together the rates of joblessness and consumer-price inflation—had fallen to levels not seen on a consistent basis since the early 1970s. In the relatively painless neighborhood of 10, the index was only about half as high as in the final years of the Carter White House.

Still more remarkable, at the close of Reagan era, was the fact that a record-high share of working-age Americans—about 63 percent—held jobs. Many analysts deemed this employment-to-population rate a truer reflection of labor-market conditions than the more widely publicized unemployment rate. At 63 percent, it was nearly 10 percentage points higher than in the mid-1950s, when unemployment in some years was below 3 percent of the labor force, a level not approached since. The reason was that in the 1950s a far smaller percentage of the working-age population sought work, and only job-seekers are counted as unemployed. More recently, as more and more women have sought work, the economy has needed to generate new jobs at a faster pace to prevent the unemployment rate from rising.

With the surge in jobs under Reagan, it was hardly a surprise that incomes—corporate as well as household—also were moving from record high to new record high. Personal income—on a per capita basis, after tax payments and adjusted for inflation—exceeded $11,000, in terms of the dollar's 1982 purchasing power, a record. This income reading was up from $9,725 only six years before, early in the Reagan presidency. Still sharper was the gain in corporate profits in the period. Approaching the $300 billion mark in 1988, the profit level had nearly doubled since 1982. On the increase as well were profit margins—profits after taxes, as a percentage of sales. The margin for manufacturing concerns, for instance, approximated 6 percent in 1988, nearly twice the comparable 1982 rate. Margins in the 6 percent area hadn't been seen since early in the post–World War II era.

Not surprisingly, the Conference Board, a nonprofit research group, reported that "U.S. consumer confidence registered an impressive gain" in 1988. The board's "consumer confidence index" jumped 7 percentage points in December 1988, to nearly 120. This was the barometer's highest reading since the late 1960s, when the U.S. economy was enjoying its longest expansion ever. "The consumer's very favorable assessment of prevailing conditions reflects the continued vigor of the economy and bodes well for the immediate future," the board declared. With unemployment down nearly to 5 percent, its lowest level in a decade and a half, with incomes on the rise, and with inflation "virtually imperceptible to the average shopper," the analysis concluded, "all these factors contribute to a high level of consumer confidence" about the economy's prospects.

A few housing statistics underscore, in a very material sense, the high general comfort level at the finish of the Reagan years. At 1,755 square feet, the median size of a single-family home in the United States had risen 15 percent in just five years, and this increase was on the heels of an 8 percent shrinkage in the preceding five-year period. Near the end of Reagan's tenure, moreover, some 23 percent of new homes had four or more bedrooms, up from 20 percent as recently as 1986, and 83 percent of the homes had at least two bathrooms, up from 80 percent in 1986. The comfort level of most Americans in Reagan's final years is all the more striking when measured within an international framework. At the time, the size of the average American home far outstripped the comparable averages in even the most advanced areas abroad. The area of floor space in the average West German dwelling came to 69 percent of the U.S. figure, and the comparable readings for France and Japan, for example, were 63 percent and 60 percent respectively.

A D D I N G to the general sense of economic well-being near the close of the Reagan presidency was a growing conviction that fears about the business outlook, in the wake of the October 1987 stock market crash, were proving false. Between August 25 and

October 19 of 1987, the stock market plunged, a drop from peak to trough of 36 percent. The 508-point collapse in the Dow Jones Industrial Average on October 19 was the steepest one-day decline in the market's history. Large declines in share prices in the past had almost always presaged an imminent recession or worse. The lone exception was a sharp drop between 1938 and 1942. There was no subsequent business slump, no doubt because huge increases in World War II military outlays bolstered an otherwise shaky economy. In every other instance when the stock market fell sharply, an economic slump ensued within no more than thirteen months.

But by December 1988, as many as fourteen recession-free months had elapsed since the market's 1987 plunge, and still the economy continued to grow briskly. The stock market, in fact, had resumed climbing since the 1987 crash, with the Dow Jones Industrial Average up about 12 percent in 1988 alone, and the rise was continuing in the opening weeks of 1989, as Bush moved into the White House.

The economy's long upswing, as 1989 began, seemed almost impervious to what had appeared only a short while earlier as ominous imbalances—the long-standing and still-enormous deficits in the federal budget and in foreign trade, and the sky-high amounts of debt in both the corporate and consumer areas. For years, many of the nation's most eminent economists—including a former chief economic adviser to Reagan, Martin Feldstein of Harvard—had been warning that these imbalances, if allowed to go on, would cripple business. Yet, as Reagan departed in January 1989, the federal budget deficit exceeded $150 billion and appeared to be on the rise again, after having ebbed for about a year. And the trade deficit, though somewhat reduced from a year earlier, remained above $100 billion and showed signs of staying in that worrisome neighborhood.

To many observers, the economy's continuing vigor was proof enough that to worry over deficits or market crashes or consumer or corporate profligacy was naive. Feldstein and other pessimists were increasingly dismissed as publicity-seeking Cassandras. If the budget and trade accounts were in deficit, no matter. No less a figure than Milton Friedman, a Nobel-laureate economist from the Hoover Institution in California and an informal adviser to

Reagan, proclaimed that the twin deficits were of little concern. Indeed, he seemed to welcome the imbalances. He charged that "media and the public have been sold a bill of goods . . . that the so-called twin deficits are time bombs." He maintained that "nothing could be further from the truth," noting that the federal debt "is a smaller fraction of the national income today than it was in any year from the end of World War II to 1960. Where were the doom-and-gloomers then?"[2] (What he did not go on to explain was that in those early postwar years the public's savings were also very high—unlike at present—and this made the debt far less burdensome. Moreover, the federal budget was piling up surpluses rather than deficits.)

As for the shortfall in trade, Friedman claimed that the trade "deficit provides dollars for [foreigners] to invest" in the United States. "It is a mystery to me," he declared, "why, to take a specific example, it is regarded as a sign of Japanese strength and U.S. weakness that the Japanese find it more attractive to invest in the U.S. than in Japan. Surely it is precisely the reverse—a sign of U.S. strength and Japanese weakness." Perhaps so. But a likelier explanation is that the Japanese had grown wary of rising U.S. protectionism under Reagan and viewed investing in the United States as a hedge against eventually being shut out of the huge U.S. market.

Friedman is widely credited with the authorship of the adage that "there is no such thing as a free lunch." As author of a collection of essays bearing that title, he pointed out, with commendable modesty, that he had merely improved the grammar in an earlier version of the same adage—that "there ain't no such thing as a free lunch." In light of Friedman's views, however, a strict grammarian must wonder whether the earlier version, with its double negative actually constituting an affirmative, did not more accurately reflect the economist's sentiments.

In any case, as the Bush presidency dawned, it seemed to many observers, besides Milton Friedman, that free lunches did indeed exist. This revelation, in fact, appeared to be the ultimate lesson of Reaganomics—that a nation could continue, year after year after year, to live beyond its means, not merely with impunity but to its considerable benefit. Federal tax rates could safely be slashed and federal spending could safely expand—and yet,

miraculously, all would turn out fine in the end, far better in fact
than if the economy had been restrained.

And yet, as Reagan's presidency ended, there were multiplying
signs, despite the evidence of economic expansion and rising
prosperity, that the general living standard of most Americans
had begun to edge down.

T H E place to begin to understand this decline is the workplace. About one in five jobs in America in the late 1980s was
part-time, a record, up from one in six a decade earlier. Such jobs,
though relatively low-paying, were fully counted in the well-publicized estimates from Washington in the late 1980s that employment was setting records. Less well known was that in 1987 alone
more than five million workers who had sought full-time jobs
were forced instead to take part-time ones.[3]

At the same time, goods-producing jobs, well paid by tradition,
accounted for a shrinking share of the labor market. Between
1979 and 1987, some 12.3 million additional jobs were generated
overall. But a breakdown shows that a 13.9 million increase in the
services category was offset by a 1.6 million drop in goods-producing jobs. To be sure, some workers in the services category
are very well paid, such as doctors and investment bankers, and
some counted within manufacturing are paid poorly, such as re-
porters for many small newspapers or magazines. But these are
exceptions. The median weekly pay in the service categories was
$344, against $398 in goods production. Among the service industries growing fastest were two where pay was especially low—
retail trade, with a median of $258 a week, and so-called service
work, from scrubbing floors to child care, at $327 a week. The
length of the average work week of employees in retail trade,
about twenty-nine hours, was thirteen hours shorter than the
average in manufacturing jobs. The average week in service
work, at thirty-two hours, was also relatively short.

Moreover, productivity stagnated in the 1980s, which hurt buying power. Imagine that a worker in a widget factory receives a
10 percent increase in his hourly pay and suppose that this
worker, by dint of greater individual effort as well as improved
plant facilities, manages to produce 10 percent more widgets each

hour on the job. As a result, the per-widget cost of his labor remains unchanged, with his higher hourly output exactly offsetting his higher hourly pay. This means, in turn, that his pay raise will not be inflationary, since the cost of producing a widget will not have climbed. And, with no new inflation, the worker's pay gain will raise his buying power, and so his standard of living will move up too.

Unfortunately, in the 1980s, hourly output gains in the private economy by and large failed to match hourly pay increases, and so per-unit labor costs rose sharply. By the late 1980s, unit labor costs were nearly twice the level of the early 1970s, as hourly pay soared some 160 percent while hourly output rose only 13 percent.[4]

The most important reason for this was industry's failure to invest sufficiently in plant and equipment to enhance productivity. Mounting drug use, rapidly changing technology, increasingly fickle customer demand, and tougher competition from abroad also hurt. Moreover, the makeup of the work force was shifting, with swift growth in two demographic groups—women and teenagers—for which productivity traditionally has lagged behind. At the same time, adult males were a shrinking component.

Another drag on productivity was the crumbling American infrastructure—highways, bridges, and the like. In the 1960s, spending on the infrastructure rose 4.5 percent annually, but in the 1970s the rate of increase fell to 1.9 percent annually and in 1980–88 to only about 1 percent. In 1988, such outlays came to less than 1 percent of the gross national product. In 1960, the government spent about $15 for every $100 that private industry spent for capital improvements, but by the mid-1980s this ratio was halved. Recently, Japan has invested 5.1 percent of its economic output in its infrastructure projects and, by no coincidence, achieved productivity growth of 3.3 percent a year. In the United States, since the late 1960s, spending on roads and bridges has fallen by roughly a third, while miles traveled in vehicles on these same roads and bridges has nearly doubled.

After a three-year study, the National Council on Public Works Improvement concluded in 1987 that "if our public works were graded on an academic scale, their recent performance would rate a scant C." Grades given were: for highways, C+; for mass transit, C—; for aviation, B—; for water resources, B; for water supply, B—; for wastewater, C; for solid waste, C—; and for hazardous waste, D. When Reagan became president, 15 percent of the nation's bridges were classified as structurally deficient, and when his two terms were over the figure was 24 percent. On the Interstate Highway System alone, 16 percent of the bridges were deemed deficient in 1988, twice the percentage six years earlier. In 1989, the Federal Highway Administration placed the cost of replacing or rebuilding shaky bridges at $50.7 billion.

The price of neglecting the infrastructure can be seen in the estimate of one large steel manufacturer requesting anonymity that it was paying at least $1 million a year in added expenses to detour its trucks some eighteen miles around a major bridge that a Midwestern state had closed rather than repair.

Such neglect affects productivity in subtle but important ways. Efficiency throughout the economy, in private as well as in public enterprises, obviously suffers if, for example, highways aren't properly maintained or airports can't carry out their flight schedules on time. Alan S. Blinder, an economics professor at Princeton University, argues convincingly that the Reagan administration may have erred when it tried to increase productivity—unsuccessfully, as it has turned out—through tax incentives for the private sector, while starving public projects. A better solution, Blinder thinks, would have been "to restore the public capital stock that has been deteriorating before our eyes."[5]

Hourly and weekly pay were by no means the only living-standard gauges to decline in the Reagan years. An inflation-adjusted index of average family income, which had more than doubled in the first three decades after World War II, fell over the next decade and a half. The decline was modest, but would have been far steeper were it not that more members within each household went to work during the period. Simply trying to maintain their families' existing living standards, women by the millions left the home and the kiddies for the labor market. The trend began before Reagan, but accelerated sharply during his presidency.

A bleak appraisal of the productivity picture and its possible impact on living standards was issued by the Conference Board soon after Reagan left office. Living standards will decline in the

1990s, it warned, unless American companies can come up with new ways to boost productivity. "All of the burden of improving our standard of living will fall on productivity, on raising worker efficiency," declared Audrey Freeman, who conducted the study for the research group. The concern was that the work force, partly for demographic reasons, would grow much more slowly in the 1990s than previously, when rising worker participation in a rapidly expanding labor force buttressed per capita income. Such a change, Ms. Freeman reckoned, could well "produce virtual stagnation in the standard of living." And this would mean, she said, that ultimately "the American pie will not be growing [and] any gains for one group in our population—for example, the Western region or the young employed—will come at the expense of other groups."

T H E dollar declined sharply, losing about half its value against Japan's yen between 1985 and 1988. The dollar's value in terms of ten major currencies dropped nearly 40 percent in the same period. Such a fall in the dollar's global worth magnifies the more modest declines in buying power resulting from inflation. If inflation is a secret tax for its subtle erosion of the dollar, the dollar's international decline is a super-secret tax. The impact may be slow to emerge but ultimately is profound, tending to raise the cost of goods and services from abroad—no minor item nowadays—while reducing the global worth of what the United States has to offer, be it goods, services, real estate, or plant facilities.

So, in a global context, living standards dropped sharply in the latter Reagan years, even though such well-publicized gauges as the gross national product kept rising. Americans who traveled abroad frequently during those years were keenly aware of this decline. Hotels and restaurants that once were well within the typical U.S. traveler's budget became prohibitive. At the same time, foreign-made goods sold in the United States, from cars to cameras, grew dearer, and increasingly the customers at the best stores and restaurants in New York or Chicago or Los Angeles were from Frankfurt or Paris or Milan or Tokyo.

The change in circumstances for Americans living and working abroad was especially pronounced. This was driven home to me when, by chance, I came upon a list of employees of American newspapers residing in London near the end of Reagan's presidency. When I had held such a job for *The Wall Street Journal* in the early 1960s, one could judge with reasonable accuracy a correspondent's status within a particular bureau by the person's London address. For example, my boss in the *Journal*'s London bureau lived in a large, comfortable apartment in Roebuck House, a block of flats in an elegant neighborhood. Britain's former foreign minister was in the apartment directly above, and from his terrace one could look out at Buckingham Palace. My London home was a somewhat smaller flat in the Hampstead section, which was a less central and slightly less fashionable part of town, but still a very attractive area.

By the late 1980s, few bureau chiefs, much less their underlings, were living in such places as Roebuck House. For most, even areas like Hampstead were too expensive. Those correspondents who carried London addresses at all were typically in areas, such as on the south side of the Thames river, that would have been unthinkable in my London years. By 1988, the only American correspondent I knew who still resided in a first-class part of town—Cadogan Place, near Sloane Square—was a fellow who had been stationed in London for over twenty years and had managed early on to secure a rent-controlled apartment.

With a stronger dollar, of course, Sloane Square addresses would have been accessible to more Americans in 1988. Between early 1985 and the middle of 1987, the period when the dollar fell most steeply, total personal income in the United States rose about $500 billion, a gain of some 15 percent. This may seem substantial, even if one takes inflation into account. But in terms of the yen, U.S. income fell more than 40 percent in 1985–87, or 492,000 billion yen.[6] For American consumers, a decline of 10 percent in the dollar's international worth in terms of other currencies is tantamount to a 10 percent tax on imported goods and services. And a deliberate effort to cheapen the dollar's value— such as the Reagan administration made in 1985—is in effect protectionism.

Meanwhile, the effort to protect U.S. textile makers under Reagan by such measures as limiting textile imports from China cost U.S. consumers some $100,000 per textile job saved, in higher prices for clothing and other textile products both domestic and imported.[7] In 1986 alone, the total cost to consumers of textile protectionism was estimated at $20.3 billion, expressed in higher import and domestic textile prices and the smaller quantity of imported items available.

The cost to consumers of restraints on Japanese cars in the Reagan years has been placed between $105,000 and $160,000 per auto job saved.[8] Attempts to protect other industries raised a wide range of prices for U.S. consumers. Quotas were imposed on imports of cheese, ice cream, and sugar. There were long bureaucratic delays in the required testing of imported office equipment. "Buy American" rules governed federal procurement of many goods and services. Special "user" fees were required for imported boats, planes, and trucks, and special environmental levies were put on imported petroleum and chemical products.

Halfway through Reagan's presidency, the hourly pay of U.S. production workers was still a standard toward which workers in other industrial countries only aspired. At $12.40 an hour, it exceeded comparable levels, expressed in dollars, in Japan ($6.35 an hour), West Germany ($9.44), Italy ($7.38), and Britain ($5.88). But by early 1988 the U.S. pay level, at $13.62, was lower than in Japan ($13.80), West Germany ($20.19), and Italy ($14.77), and only modestly higher than in Britain ($11.06), whose pay rate only four years earlier had been less than half the U.S. level.[9]

H O M E O W N E R S H I P still plays a major role in the American dream, and as we have noted, the size of the typical single-family home did expand considerably in the Reagan years, dwarfing homes in nations whose economies grew faster than the U.S. economy. But in 1988, a thirty-year-old American buying a home spent 41 percent of his or her yearly income, on the average, for mortgage payments, real estate taxes, and insurance. In 1958, the comparable rate was 14 percent. And while the average U.S. home was far larger than its overseas counterpart in 1988, the expense of maintaining that home was also greater than in most other countries. The average rental cost in the United States for a two-bedroom apartment, for example, came to nearly 40 percent of household earnings, against only 23 percent in Japan.[10]

In 1979, some 44 percent of Americans between the ages of twenty-five and twenty-nine owned their homes. Near the end of Reagan's presidency, this rate was down to 36 percent. In the same years, the down payment of the typical U.S. home buyer rose from about one-third of his or her annual income to more than one-half. Working couples whose combined incomes exceeded $100,000 were beginning in the 1980s to find themselves unable to afford the same quality of housing that their parents had afforded a generation before on much smaller incomes. Paul S. Hewitt, in his mid-thirties, reported in *The Washington Post* that his and his wife's combined earnings totaled $115,000, enough to place them in the top 5 percent of U.S. families. Yet, the Hewitts were finding themselves virtually priced out of the sorts of "nice, suburban neighborhoods" into which they wished to buy. His parents, he recalled, bought their Oakland, California, home in 1958 for just $28,000, which would be equal to $113,000 in 1988. With an interest rate of 6 percent, the parents' monthly costs came to $122. In 1988, Hewitt reckoned, the same house would sell for about $700,000 and, with 20 percent paid down and a fixed-rate mortgage, the monthly expense would be somewhere around $4,500. To qualify for such a mortgage, a 1988 buyer would have to earn well above $200,000. In contrast, Hewitt recalled, "my dad, who at the time was younger than I am now, qualified for his mortgage with an annual income of less than $6,000."[11]

In the 1980s, homeownership declined in the United States for every age group under fifty-four years. For all Americans, the high point in homeownership—at nearly 66 percent—was reached in 1980, just before Reagan took office. By the end of his tenure, the rate had fallen below 64 percent, less than in the early 1970s. "Homeownership has not become less desirable, it has become less affordable," concluded a 1988 study. With a more than doubling of the mortgage delinquency rate during the Reagan years, the report added, "even those who can afford to buy their own home are having more trouble keeping up the payments."[12]

Much of the housing in such major metropolitan areas as New

York, Honolulu, Los Angeles, Boston, and San Francisco had grown unaffordable for most Americans by the end of Reagan's presidency. A national survey estimated the amount of income necessary to purchase a median-cost home in each U.S. metropolitan area and compared this with the median family income in each area. By dividing the latter number by the former, an "affordability" ratio was constructed. This ratio for the New York area stood at 0.54 in 1988, the lowest in the nation. New York's median family income was $31,948, and the income needed to buy a home there was $58,887; by no coincidence, New York also showed the highest median home price, $190,500. In 1980, by comparison, the median family income in New York was $25,000, but the median price of a home was only $77,100. Other affordability ratios deemed painfully low included 0.63 in Honolulu, 0.68 in Los Angeles, 0.69 in Boston, and 0.72 in San Francisco.[13]

Meeting in San Francisco in November 1988, the National Association of Realtors reported that for the nation as a whole, the average first-time home buyer had only 77 percent of the income needed to qualify for a mortgage on a "starter" home of average price, which was estimated at $76,670. The association also found that the "affordability gap" between the relatively young first-time home buyers and home buyers in general was the widest in the thirteen years that such data had been kept. The typical first-time home buyer, it was reckoned, would have to pay a monthly mortgage fee of $583, which would require an annual income of almost $28,000, about $6,000 above the actual median income for first-time buyers.

Under Reagan, moreover, federal funds available to subsidize low-income rentals and for public housing were repeatedly slashed. At about $28 billion in 1981, the totals by the end of his eight years were down to $10 billion. Over the same period, the number of households below the poverty level rose sharply.

In the 1980s, a growing number of adult children lived briefly on their own but then returned to the parental nest. Rising housing costs were largely to blame, but there were also many young people who had been reared in affluence and then ventured out on their own. But when they encountered the real world, they returned to the nest. Twenty percent of twenty-five-to-twenty-nine-year-olds were living at home with their parents at the end of Reagan's presidency, nearly twice the percentage in the previous decade.

In this regard, I recall attending a party at the Manhattan apartment of old friends who were celebrating the arrival of their first grandchild. On prominent display for the guests were the couple's daughter, a woman in her late twenties, and her infant daughter, the grandchild, both newly arrived on a brief visit from London, where the young husband was at work for the English branch of an American bank. But also much in evidence at the party was our friends' son, the new mother's younger brother, a strapping, able fellow several years out of Harvard and employed as a paralegal at a large, prosperous New York law firm. While complimenting him on his yeoman service in repeatedly passing around the hors d'oeuvres, I asked where he was living. He replied that he had not, in fact, been able to find a suitable place that he could afford and so had persuaded his parents to take him back in. "I'm living here, in my old room," he said. "It costs me nothing and leaves me free to spend my salary on a lot of things that wouldn't otherwise be possible, but I miss the independence of having my own place."

Such arrangements may increase the comfort and affluence of the young people returning to the nest, but they also can make conditions less comfortable for parents, such as my friends, who had felt that they had made a good effort at parenting and now it would be over.

Since even to rent a place was difficult for many young people, such as the young man from Harvard, it is no wonder as the Reagan presidency wound down that more and more American families could no longer take the dream of eventual homeownership for granted. Indeed, the Reagan years marked the first period since the 1930s, the years of the Great Depression, in which there was a sustained decline in homeownership. The hunger of Americans to own a home had not diminished, but to try to keep the dream alive more and more people were compelled to travel farther and farther from home to work and back again each day—a difficult situation. And increasingly these sojourns took place on clogged highways and aboard trains that were poorly maintained and behind schedule, a further erosion of living conditions.

T H E R E is more to the American dream, of course, than owning a home. There is the belief that prosperity, based on individual initiative, will be shared widely enough so that even the least productive citizens may subsist reasonably well. But as the Reagan years passed, this was hardly the situation, and perhaps the starkest sign of failure was the nation's proliferating homeless population. From the mid-1970s through Reagan's presidency, some 4.5 million units of low-income housing simply "disappeared from our nation's inventory," according to David O. Maxwell, chairman and chief executive officer of the Federal National Mortgage Association, who called the homeless "the most visible manifestation" of this "housing shame." He added that the expiration of remaining federal subsidies for low-income housing, proposed by the outgoing Reagan administration, "threatens hundreds of thousands more units in the years immediately ahead."[14]

A sobering statistic: At the end of Reagan's tenure, more than a third of America's homeless were families rather than individual men and women. Under Reagan, federal subsidies for new low-income housing fell by some 60 percent, and total federal outlays for housing fell from over $30 billion to about $8 billion. In New York City alone, federal support fell $7 billion. In the 1970s, some twenty thousand federally supported homes were built yearly, while with Reagan the annual number plunged to five thousand. By 1989, there was an eighteen-year wait to get into public housing in New York City. At the time, the city's Human Resources Administration issued a statistical sketch of New York's homeless families: 95 percent were black or Hispanic; 86 percent were headed by women; teenagers made up 11 percent of the group, whose average age was twenty-seven years; 50 percent of the children were under five years old; and 83 percent of the families were on welfare.

No one knows the number of homeless in the nation as a whole when Reagan left office. But there seems little question that their population was in the high hundreds of thousands, if not in the low millions as some estimates show. Whatever the true number, there could be little question that homelessness had grown swiftly. In New York City, where I live, by the late 1980s I found it impossible to walk more than a block or two in mid-Manhattan without encountering shabbily clothed men and women camping on sidewalks; many appeared reasonably cogent and simply down on their luck, while others were deranged and in need of psychiatric care. Mid-Manhattan was dismaying for anyone cherishing the egalitarian promise of the American dream. Ostentation and poverty appeared side by side. Nor was Manhattan unique. Ever-longer stretch limousines alongside tattered street dwellers were increasingly common from Miami to San Francisco, from Boston to Los Angeles, though by 1990 the business of building stretch limousines had also fallen on hard times.

The share of total personal income received by the poorest 20 percent of the population fell 11 percent, adjusted for inflation, in Reagan's first six years, according to the Commerce Department, while the share received by the top 20 percent rose 14 percent. The top group collected 44 percent of all income, compared with less than 5 percent for the bottom group. And a more detailed breakdown by the Congressional Budget Office turns up even greater disparities. From the late 1970s to 1988, the poorest 10 percent of families suffered an 11 percent decline in family income, adjusted for inflation and taxes, while the richest 5 percent enjoyed a 37 percent gain in income. Sharper still was the 74 percent rise in income for the top 1 percent of families. By 1990, the nonprofit Center on Budget and Policy Priorities estimates, the top 2.5 million earners were taking in as much income as the 100 million lowest paid.

In approximately the same period, the median income of black families fell some 5 percent, while that of white families gained 1 percent. At about 13 percent, the national poverty rate was nearly a percentage point higher than two decades before. The total of about 32.5 million poverty-ridden Americans had risen by about 8 million since the late 1970s. And, lamentably, poverty was most widespread among children under six; 22 percent were below the poverty line, compared with 18 percent before Reagan came to Washington. About 45 percent of black children were in poverty and about 38 percent of Hispanic children. And poverty was far more widespread among American children than among children in other industrial nations where comparable statistics were available. The child poverty rate was only 5 percent in Switzerland and Sweden, 8 percent in West Germany, 9 percent in Canada, and 10 percent in Britain. "It makes you really sit up and take notice when you realize that children in the United States have poverty rates two and three times those of other industrial nations for which we have comparable data," commented Isabel Sawhill, an economist at the Urban Institute, a Washington research group.[15]

A poll in October 1988 found sharp disagreement among Americans over Reagan's impact on their financial circumstances. They were asked not simply how things were going, as in the Gallup Poll cited earlier, but whether they were financially better or worse off as a result of Reagan's policies. Of the respondents deemed wealthy, 75 percent said that they were better off. But all other categories of Americans interviewed—the middle class, low-income people, the young, blacks, and even the elderly— leaned in the opposite direction. Only 26 percent of the low-income group believed their lot had improved under Reagan, while 60 percent claimed it had worsened. Among blacks, 31 percent reported an improvement, while 43 percent found things to be worse, and similar patterns were evident in the other demographic groups.[16]

Tax laws added to the inequity. They were far more burdensome for lower-income families than for the rich. In early 1989, the nonprofit Tax Foundation issued a report concluding that "low-income families pay out a much larger share of income as excise taxes than do the average- or high-income families." It reckoned that the overall "sales and excise tax burden is over five times greater for the lowest-income families than for the highest." The total tax burden, including state and local levies, was nearly twice as high—26 percent of income—for taxpayers earning less than $10,000 as for those with incomes above $90,000. The Social Security tax system, with its cutoff point for higher incomes, was also regressive, of course, and the Tax Reform Act of 1986, remarkably, imposed a lower marginal tax rate on the wealthiest people than on those earning somewhat less. Under the law, for example, a person earning $150,000 paid an added $330 in taxes for a $1,000 pay increase, while someone earning $1 million paid only $280 for a similar increase.

During the Reagan years, *Forbes* magazine began publishing annual lists of those whom it reckoned to be the richest four hundred Americans. With each new list, the number of billionaires rapidly increased. The wealth of the *Forbes* 400 roughly matched the savings that all Americans had in commercial banks and far exceeded the federal budget deficit, which was above $200 billion during much of the Reagan presidency. Under Reagan, the wealthiest 10 percent of the population controlled nearly 70 percent of the nation's wealth, up from 64 percent a quarter century earlier.[17] If one excludes the value of homes lived in by their owners—the major source of wealth for most Americans— the concentration was even greater. The richest 10 percent owned 83 percent of all private wealth, and the top 0.5 percent, fewer than 1.5 million people, owned two and a half times as much as the 212 million people in the bottom 90 percent of the population.

An extreme illustration of the sums being made by Wall Street lawyers, for example, was the fee of $20 million charged by Wachtell, Lipton, Rosen & Katz, the law firm representing Kraft Inc. in that firm's takeover in 1988 by Philip Morris. Wachtell Lipton lawyers spent only two weeks on the deal, which works out to about $5,000 an hour, assuming round-the-clock labors by twenty-four lawyers. Listing the one hundred people on Wall Street who earned the most in 1987, *Financial World* magazine placed a thirty-three-year-old trader named Paul Tudor Jones II at the top, with earnings for the year of between $80 million and $100 million. Within a single Wall Street investment firm, Goldman, Sachs & Co., there were forty-eight partners whose pay ranged from a low of $4 million to a high of "at least" $32 million. Within manufacturing, *Fortune* magazine reported that Lee Iacocca, chairman of Chrysler Corp., received $17,656,000 in 1987. This dwarfed the pay of Iacocca's counterparts abroad, such as Edzard Reuter of Daimler-Benz in West Germany, with estimated earnings of $1,200,000, and Tadashi Kume of Honda in Japan, with estimated earnings of $450,000. In 1988, Standard & Poor's reported, the average compensation of the 708 highest-paid U.S. executives was $2,025,485, or ninety-three times the average pay of a factory worker and seventy-two times that of a school-teacher. Two decades earlier, by comparison, the average for chief executives was forty-one times that for factory workers and thirty-eight times that for schoolteachers.

The patterns that emerged under Reagan were very far from the egalitarianism of the American dream. While the rich grew richer, over 20 percent of American children lived in poverty, and the rate was rising. A *Business Week* cover story on May 1, 1989, focused on the new heights to which chief executives' pay had soared in Reagan's final year, but elsewhere in the issue the magazine's economics editor, Karen Pennar, reported that much of the nation's new wealth wasn't "trickling down" and blamed "the evisceration of antipoverty and job-training programs during the Reagan administration." Meanwhile, the cover story reported that the two top executives of Disney Corp. together took home over $70 million in 1988.

C R I M E spread rapidly during the Reagan presidency, so that by the late 1980s there were 8.6 murders, 37.5 rapes, and 225.1 robberies each year per every 100,000 Americans. The comparable rates abroad were sharply lower. A few examples: in West Germany, 4.5 murders, 9.2 rapes, and 46.8 robberies per 100,000 citizens; in France, 4.4 murders, 5.3 rapes, and 91.8 robberies; in Britain, 4.3 murders, 10.4 rapes, and 60.1 robberies; in Japan, 1.4 murders, 1.4 rapes, and 1.6 robberies. In 1988 alone, 20,680 Americans were murdered, one every twenty-five minutes. A woman resident of New York City would have had about ten times more green walking space than her Tokyo counterpart as the Reagan era ended, but was six times likelier to be murdered, twenty-five times likelier to be raped, and 140 times likelier to be robbed. Moreover, a robber was three times likelier to be caught in Japan than in the United States. In England, with about 20 percent of the population of the United States, there were 3 percent the number of murders.

A sign of the time was the situation in New Haven, Connecticut, a city with growing numbers of poor black and Hispanic families, as well as several thousand of the nation's brightest young people, students at Yale University, many of them from affluent, white households. The New Haven scene in the Reagan years was such that the university was obliged to publish in its weekly "bulletin and calendar" a regular report pointing out for students on a map of the campus precisely where each month's "crimes against persons" had occurred. The report for the period from October 16 to November 16, 1988, for example, showed these on-campus crimes: eighteen robberies, seventeen assaults, two rapes, and one attempted rape. Seven of these crimes against Yale students occurred, the map showed, on a single block in the heart of Yale's campus.

The increased use, particularly among the poor, of such highly addictive drugs as crack clearly fueled the spread of crime in the latter Reagan years, and this might have happened whoever was in the White House. But the spread might have been less swift under a president less bent on cutting tax rates at the top brackets and more concerned with channeling federal funds, whether directly or through states and localities, into carrying on the drug war in a more serious, sensible way.

During Reagan's presidency, the nation's capital, of all places, was also its most crime-ridden city. In his last four years in office, the number of murders within the District of Columbia rose from 148 in 1985, to 197 in 1986, to 228 in 1987, and to 372 in 1988. On an average day in 1988, the city experienced 160 crimes, from murder to rape to robbery. In early 1989, Washington's police chief, Maurice T. Turner, Jr., told an audience at the National Press Club there that his best hope, to reverse the trend, was for medical researchers to develop "an inoculation to prevent a person from getting a euphoria from using drugs."[18] In August 1990, the Senate Judiciary Committee estimated that a record 23,220 people would be murdered over the course of the year, about two thousand more than in 1989.

Most crime is committed by people in their teens and twenties, and in the 1980s this group increasingly was without parental supervision from the very early years. This, in turn, reflected how hard it was becoming for families to maintain living standards and stay together. When Reagan took office, mothers worked in 51 percent of wage-earning families, but when his presidency ended this rate was near 60 percent. In the same period, the percentage of preschool children with working mothers swelled from 43 percent to about 56 percent.

While crime rose, the nation's health care, once a source of considerable national pride, was a matter of increasing disappointment.

About 90 percent of 1,250 adult Americans surveyed believed that the U.S. system of health care required a basic overhaul, and the rest felt that the system functioned only "pretty well." The comparable approval rate in Canada, with a national health-insurance system, was 56 percent and in Britain, with a fully nationalized system, 27 percent. Americans with incomes under $15,000 a year, the poll found, visited a doctor fewer times a year than their foreign counterparts and were significantly less satisfied with such visits. Only 54 percent of Americans were "very satisfied" with visits to doctors, against a satisfaction rate of 73 percent in Canada and 63 percent in Britain. While 63 percent of the Americans favored a health-care system like that in Canada, only 3 percent of the Canadians and 12 percent of the Britons said they would prefer the U.S. system to their own systems. Dr. Robert Blendon, chairman of the department of health policy and management at the Harvard School of Public Health and director of the study, concluded that it "confirms all of one's worst fears about the American system: We have the most expensive, the least well-liked, the least equitable and in many ways the most inefficient system."[19]

The U.S. system in the Reagan years included, of course, government health insurance for the elderly, the poor, and the disabled, as well as varying degrees of employer-supported insurance in private businesses. But there was little or no provision for the millions of other Americans who did not fall within such categories. As many as 37 million Americans were without health insurance, many more were underinsured, and nearly half of those below the poverty line were not covered by Medicaid, aimed mainly at welfare recipients.

Other signs of decline were evident as well. The cost of an education soared in the Reagan years, with the average college tuition rising from $3,603 to $6,175 at public institutions and from $6,665 to $12,511 at private ones.[20] Yet, educational standards were deteriorating. Of 3.8 million American youths turned eighteen in 1988, some 700,000 had dropped out of high school, and a like number who did graduate could not even read their diplomas. In a thirteen-nation comparison of achievement, American high-school seniors were ranked at the bottom in biology, eleventh in chemistry, and ninth in physics. The illiteracy rate among minority students, who will make up more than half of school-age Americans by the end of this century, exceeded 20 percent in Reagan's final year. The dropout rate among U.S. high-schoolers was more than double that in Japan, and the rate for American black males was nearly triple. And the dropout rate for young American blacks and Hispanics was, respectively, 35 percent and 45 percent. For young Americans who remained in school, the school year was 180 days long, on the average, while that of their counterparts in Japan was 240 days.

American living standards, in sum, deteriorated in crucial ways during Reagan's presidency, and it is remarkable that the decline did not bring more attention in the media or concern at the ballot box. That it did not was in large measure a tribute to an old, appealing actor's undiminished Hollywood skills.

CHAPTER THREE

A TROUBLED LEGACY

Why hasn't the American dream come true? Why have so many things gone wrong? Lacking an objective understanding of social life, people imagine themselves in the grip of uncontrolled Satanic forces. But we, ordinary men and women, are the sole authors of our discontents. Seeking a better world, step by step, we have spun the web that holds us from our dreams.
—Marvin Harris, *America Now* (1981)

T H E R E was nothing mysterious about what had harmed the economy during Reagan's years in the White House and posed such a challenge for Bush. It was well recognized in Washington as well as among business planners from New York to Los Angeles that the United States had a productivity problem, brought on by a combination of too much borrowing, too little saving, and too much spending on such nonproductive areas as defense, interest on debt, and various entitlements—as opposed to spending that would eventually strengthen the economy, such as for new plant and equipment, education, and the like. But habits of long standing are usually difficult to break, no matter how detrimental. This is especially so when a habit produces considerable temporary comfort.

An attempt to sustain the short-run comfort level was hardly unique to Reagan's presidency. But Reagan's complacency was reinforced by the dubious economics of a free lunch—the notion that lasting prosperity required little more than a fat cut in federal tax rates.

This idea, not surprisingly, was extraordinarily popular at the ballot box, promising increased prosperity at reduced expense. Business activity, spurred by tax-cutting, would generate such a surge in earnings that tax revenues would surge as well, even with reduced tax rates. Far from deepening, the budget deficit would narrow and disappear.

By the end of Reagan's two terms, the federal deficit remained enormous. Though down from the record $221 billion level of fiscal 1986, it was running at an annual rate of more than $160 billion when Reagan left office, still high and suggesting that the free lunch was proving to be somewhat less appetizing and less free than advertised. Yet, as the economic expansion rolled on and unemployment kept dropping, policymakers not surprisingly avoided the difficult steps, such as raising taxes and curbing spending, that would have brought the budget closer to balance. And they gained support from a number of prominent economists, both left and right of the political center, who argued that the perennial budget deficits, if not a boon, were at least irrelevant to the economy's good health.

A *Forbes* magazine editorial by M. S. Forbes, Jr., the late publisher's son and successor and, like his father, a staunch supporter of prosperity through tax cuts, noted that Washington, through legislative action, had already declared many spending items, from U.S. Postal Service losses to Farm Credit System costs, to be "off-budget"—that is, not a part of the regular federal budget whose well-publicized deficits were subject under the Gramm-Rudman-Hollings Act to yearly ceilings. "Why not go all the way," Forbes asked, only half in jest, "and proclaim the entire deficit an off-budget expense?"[1]

Milton Friedman, who served as an informal adviser to Reagan, was by no means the only eminent economist to play down the deficit. Robert Heilbroner and Peter Bernstein, in other regards frequent critics of Reagan's economic policies, argued that perhaps Americans were overly concerned by the budget's chronic imbalances. "Reducing the deficit," they maintained, was far less urgent than supposed. In itself, the deficit was not particularly worrisome in their view, and it became so only when it reflected a frivolous use of federal revenues.[2]

Robert Eisner, an economics professor at Northwestern University, argued in a similar vein that the federal budget was in far better shape than the government's numbers indicated. He partly blamed what he deemed to be inappropriate federal accounting procedures, which regarded investments as expenses and failed to account for the extent to which inflation eroded the value of what the government owed.[3] Analysts at the Institute for Research on the Economics of Taxation in Washington also argued that it was silly to worry much about the deficit, since it was "financed out of the pool of saving generated around the world," and with such "a global pool of saving to be tapped" the deficit was not a problem. "There really is no imperative to solve the budget problem," the report concluded.[4]

The attitude that deficits didn't matter reached a high point of sorts in the February 1989 issue of *Atlantic* magazine. Titled "Is the Deficit Really So Bad?" the cover story stressed that "none of the bad things the deficit was supposed to cause has happened yet" and questioned whether they ever would. So Reagan's deficits, it argued, "enabled the country, without an offsetting tax increase, to build up its defenses and to continue to pay for programs that distribute benefits" to the populace.[5]

Conservatives such as Friedman and Forbes and liberals such as Heilbroner and Eisner favored deficits for their own idealogical reasons. To the conservatives, deficits meant protection against new federal spending initiatives by a government strapped for revenues. Meanwhile, many liberals viewed perennial deficits as a tolerable consequence of governmental efforts to maintain an expanding economy and to sustain needier folk through federal social programs; they regarded the Reagan deficits as less evil than a recession or cutbacks in aid.

B U T deficits do matter. Deficits encourage consumption and depress aggregate savings, the very trends that weakened the American economy in the Reagan years. Deficits increase consumption, because, as government expenditures exceed revenues, federal money flows to consumers; the Treasury pays out more than it takes in. And deficits reduce savings, since they compel the government to borrow from a savings pool that would otherwise be more fully available for presumably more productive projects in private industry. Foreign savings inflows, it should be noted, have helped the government to fill its borrowing needs, but in the process, as we have seen, the United States has lost a good deal of economic independence. Federal outlays can be used to enhance productivity, to be sure, but this rarely happens and certainly did not under Reagan, as the woeful neglect of the nation's public infrastructure in those years testifies. In the main, the spending was for the military, various entitlement programs, and interest charges on the federal debt, which swelled with Reagan's deficits.

The argument was often made by the Reagan White House that large deficits were also evident in relatively vigorous economies abroad. In terms of overall economic activity, governmental deficit levels in 1988 were nearly as high in Japan and West Germany, for example, as in the United States. If such nations could retain their competitive vigor despite such deficits, why not the United States? One reason why not was that in the United States the rate of savings was generally far lower than overseas, and financing a deficit tends, of course, to weigh less heavily when savings are plentiful. Another factor was that in the United States, more than overseas, the deficits were largely used for purposes other than to improve productivity. Maintaining the infrastructure, for instance, was generally accorded a higher priority in the Japanese and West German budgets than in the U.S. budget.

Those who minimized the deficits of the Reagan years tended to overlook a crucial relationship that has existed over the decades between the federal budget and the business cycle. Budget deficits usually narrow and even occasionally disappear over the course of expansion phases of the business cycle. In part, this is because, as expansions progress, unemployment and economic hardship diminish, reducing the need for relief programs. The pattern also reflects the fact that individual and corporate earnings normally rise in expansions, and this in turn helps increase federal tax revenues. Deficits usually deepen substantially during recessions. As unemployment increases and earnings erode, the government spends more and takes in less.

The magnitude of these trends can be seen in the explosion of the budget deficit during the 1981–82 recession, a sixteen-month downturn in which the unemployment rate moved above 10 percent for the first time since the end of World War II. In July 1981, when the recession began, the deficit was running at an annual rate of $50 billion, some $25 billion less than a year earlier. In November 1982, when the recession finally hit bottom, the deficit was just over $200 billion, a fourfold rise in sixteen months. Earlier postwar recessions saw a similar pattern, often with even sharper increases, though in absolute numbers the deficits, like the economy itself, were smaller.

In late 1988, the deficit was running at a rate of about $160 billion annually, some $80 billion below the record level of mid-1986, and the White House understandably made much of the improvement. There was even talk that the budget problem, if ever there had been one, appeared finally to be over. But this overlooked the long-standing relationship between the budget and the business cycle. A declining deficit of $160 billion is one thing within the context of a long cyclical expansion; after some six years of economic growth, the deficit should indeed have been narrowing as Reagan's presidency neared an end. But such a deficit is quite another matter after years of expansion when a new recession is possible, for if one applies the reasonably typical pattern of the 1981–82 slump—when the deficit quadrupled—a deficit of $640 billion, a staggering sum, looms ahead. The economy was not entering a recession in 1988, but it was disingenuous for Reagan and his supporters to disregard the impact of the business cycle and suggest, with the deficit still near $160 billion, that this was no longer a serious concern.

This attitude was in keeping with Reagan's perennial forecasts—always misleading—of vast budgetary improvement just ahead. For 1982, he initially predicted a deficit of $45 billion. The actual deficit turned out to be $127.9 billion. For 1983, he forecast $91.5 billion, and the final figure was $207.8 billion. And so it went through his two terms, so that over the full eight years the actual deficits cumulatively came to about $355 billion more than he originally predicted. Preoccupied with the news of the moment, the Washington press corps by and large paid little notice to just how far off the mark these forecasts invariably turned out to be.

By the time the actual numbers were available, the predictions, though well publicized when they were issued from the White House, had long been forgotten.

Number juggling also played a role. The Gramm-Rudman-Hollings Act, which Congress passed with a White House blessing in 1985, set progressively lower limits on the size of the deficit. Its passage indicated, at least at first glance, the adoption of a tougher fiscal policy, but in fact the legislation was largely a sham.

Ostensibly, it mandated across-the-board budget-cutting if its yearly deficit targets were not met. However, as an offset to federal expenditures, Gramm-Rudman-Hollings counted Social Security funds, which theoretically were set aside for a projected surge of retirees—the post–World War II baby boomers—early in the twenty-first century. This procedure served, of course, to reduce sharply the yearly deficits for purposes of meeting Gramm-Rudman-Hollings limits. In practice, Social Security taxes were collected and beneficiaries paid their entitlements, and the remaining money was added to general federal revenues and subsequently spent on sundry military and social projects. When the Treasury Department spent this surplus, it simply made a bookkeeping entry to the effect that it owed a particular amount to the Social Security Trust Fund, creating in effect a nonnegotiable IOU. Even interest due was a bookkeeping entry, affirming that the Treasury owed such-and-such to the fund. Under this gimmickry, projections showed that the Social Security fund would hold some $12 trillion in Treasury IOUs by the year 2030, when retirements should surge among the big post–World War II baby-boom generation. But how can retirees be paid with IOUs? The Treasury would have to sell huge amounts of new bonds to redeem the IOUs, raise taxes precipitously, cut retirement benefits sharply, or engage in some combination of these unpleasant alternatives.

In the 1980s, moreover, vast amounts of federal spending were placed off-budget, though not to the extent suggested by Forbes. By early 1989, the deficit for purposes of Gramm-Rudman-Hollings came to just over $160 billion annually, but this conveniently included nearly $50 billion of surplus Social Security money. Without this sum, the deficit was over $210 billion.

But even this was understated, for it overlooked enormous off-budget outlays by various federal agencies. The growth of these off-budget expenditures under Reagan was awesome. In 1980, they totaled $39.5 billion, against $576.7 billion of on-budget spending. By 1989, the off-budget total reached a record $210.9 billion, up 433 percent. By comparison, on-budget outlays reached $926.2 billion, also a record, but the rate of gain was a relatively modest 60 percent. This off-budget surge resulted largely from worthless and below-cost loans incurred by such large agencies as the Federal Home Loan Mortgage Corp. as well as many smaller government-backed institutions like the Student Loan Marketing Association and the College Construction Loan Insurance Corp.

The taxpayers' bill for foreclosures on federally backed mortgages for middle-class housing alone passed $2 billion in mid-1989. The Federal Housing Administration, which provides federal insurance on loans of home buyers, lost $452 million, and the Government National Mortgage Association, the mortgage-financing agency known as Ginnie Mae, showed losses of over $50 million. The agency blamed much of its problem on guarantees of unsound loans by yet another federal agency, the Department of Veterans Affairs. In the last four years of Reagan's presidency, the VA received $1.7 billion from the Treasury to keep its loan fund above water.

With these agency outlays also counted, the true overall deficit totaled more than $284 billion when Reagan left office, nearly double the Gramm-Rudman-Hollings deficit target for Reagan's last year. This was a record, higher even than in mid-1986, when the deficit, as officially stated for Gramm-Rudman-Hollings, was at its peak. So, measured honestly, the deficit actually increased even in the final years of Reagan's presidency.

From 1984 to 1986, for example, the Farm Credit System lost nearly $5 billion in bad loans and required off-budget transfusions of some $4 billion to stay alive. Its debt obligations, backed by federal guarantees, along with the obligations of similar off-budget enterprises, totaled an estimated $1 trillion near the end of Reagan's presidency.

In early 1989, Charles A. Bowsher, the head of the General Accounting Office, an investigative arm of Congress, concluded that the deficit situation was far worse than it was being portrayed. His comment followed White House forecasts that the deficit would be cut to $100 billion or less by 1990. Bowsher called such talk misleading and estimated that a more accurate figure would be nearer $300 billion. "Everyone knows the numbers are fudged and that they never reflect reality," he said. "I think you've got to reform the whole budget process."[6]

The $100 billion official forecast also rested on such assumptions as interest rates of 5.5 percent in the coming year, lower than most economists anticipated, and overall economic growth of 3.5 percent, higher than generally expected. The official forecast also assumed revenues of some $24 billion from such one-time sources as future asset sales, often projected at unrealistically high prices. In a joint statement, two Democratic senators, Herb Kohl of Wisconsin and Charles S. Robb of Virginia, summed up the situation this way: "Our collective credibility is being eroded by the deficits of the 1980s. Americans know we've missed every Gramm-Rudman-Hollings target . . . we've ever set."

GRAMM–RUDMAN–HOLLINGS reflected a leadership vacuum in Washington. Swiftly enacted, it placed a supposed automatic—and anonymous—brake on federal spending if its targets were exceeded. Without it, politicians voting against new spending programs or to cut old ones would have been forced to stand up and be counted. Figures released in mid-1989 by the Congressional Budget Office showed that the budget deficit, as calculated for Gramm-Rudman-Hollings purposes, would exceed the law's $100 billion target ceiling for fiscal 1990 by $10 billion, or $4 billion more than was allowed, at least in theory, before the implementation of automatic, across-the-board spending cuts in domestic and military projects. But not to worry, for under the toothless law it was up to the White House's Office of Management and Budget to determine whether the ceiling would actually be breached, and the administration's position, maintained with a straight face, was that the deficit would remain under the legal limit.

Meanwhile, with Reagan's enthusiastic support, Bush reaffirmed repeatedly his campaign pledge not to raise taxes. Among the primary contenders in 1988, the only one who proposed new taxes was Bruce Babbitt, a former Arizona governor and a Democrat. He proposed a national consumption tax among others, but in mid-February, after a sorry fifth-place finish in the Iowa caucuses and a sorrier sixth place in the New Hampshire primary, Babbitt abandoned the presidential race. His rivals stamped his tax ideas "regressive," and when he withdrew he observed ruefully that "we are still, on both sides, running a presidential campaign that is avoiding reality, and we can't have an honest dialogue about the changes we need." Babbitt's failure spoke for itself. The voters wanted no new taxes.

A similar aversion to painful but necessary measures was the Reagan administration's decision to seek a cheaper dollar in foreign-exchange markets. The U.S. trade account was hemorrhaging at an unsustainable rate in 1985, when the dollar had peaked against other leading currencies. Entire industries seemed dead or dying as demand surged at home for imported merchandise and dwindled abroad for American goods. A better remedy than devaluation, but a politically difficult one, would have been to constrain consumption, even at the risk of a recession, and to spur saving and ultimately productivity. What the administration chose instead was to weaken the dollar and reduce the price to foreigners of American goods, services, production facilities, and real estate. Thus fundamental measures were put off, but the effect on American consumers was soon evident, even though a costlier TV set from Japan impinges far more subtly on living standards than a tax increase to curb consumption. Meanwhile, many American exporters chose to raise prices as the dollar fell, rather than try to hold their prices down and increase their market shares abroad. In December 1988, U.S. export prices on average were 10 percent higher than a year before.

In the spring of 1989, the Bank for International Settlements lamented Washington's refusal to bring the budget into closer balance. The bank's annual report warned that "the case for using whatever measures are available to reduce the United States federal deficit has been made so often and so convincingly that the lack of significant further progress is deplorable." The Swiss-based international bank, whose members include central bankers around the world, urged particularly that U.S. leaders restrain consumption at both the consumer and governmental levels.

But such measures were steadfastly eschewed. Instead, the Reagan years witnessed, for example, a near-doubling of the budget for the Department of Education, which the president had promised to abolish along with the Department of Energy. Between 1981 and 1987, federal spending for entitlement programs rose about 140 percent, to nearly $500 billion a year. Much of this money no doubt was well-spent, but much was little more than welfare for the well-off. In fiscal 1986, about 85 percent of entitlement outlays—for programs ranging from farm-price supports to Social Security—required no means test for recipients. Jobless millionaires, still clipping their coupons and cashing their dividend checks, could collect unemployment compensation as readily as anyone else. In 1986, for example, sixty-five of 35,875 personal tax returns showing gross earnings of at least $1 million also showed at least some income from unemployment compensation. Peter G. Peterson, a former Secretary of Commerce, calculated that "the unearned benefits enjoyed by wealthy recipients are far greater than the unearned benefits enjoyed by poor recipients."[7]

Particularly egregious was the case of Marc Rich, an American residing in Switzerland, with a multicount indictment against him in the United States for income-tax fraud. A congressional committee reported in early 1989 that some $65 million in grain export subsidies had been paid to a commodities firm with apparent ties to Rich. The firm was one of twenty large commodities outfits partaking in a federal "export enhancement program" paying out nearly $800 million a year, the difference between U.S. and world price levels.

To change all this would have required a political leadership willing to take on an electorate whose mood was well characterized in a speech by Senator Fritz Hollings of South Carolina, who helped draft Gramm-Rudman-Hollings. Using the acronyms of the entitlement world, Hollings, a Democrat, recounted the hypothetical history of a Korean War veteran. The man returned from Korea, went to college on the GI Bill, bought his house with an FHA loan, saw his children born in a VA hospital, started a business with an SBA loan, got electricity from TVA and, later, water from an EPA project. His parents retired to a farm on Social Security, got electricity from REA and soil testing from USDA. When the father became ill, the family was saved from financial ruin by Medicare and a life was saved with a drug developed through NIH. The children participated in the school lunch program, learned physics from teachers trained in an NSF program, and went through college with guaranteed student loans. The veteran drove to work on the Interstate and moored his boat in a channel dredged by Army engineers. When floods hit, he took Amtrak to Washington to apply for disaster relief, and spent some time in the Smithsonian museums. Then one day he wrote his congressman an angry letter asking the government to get off his back and complaining about paying taxes for all those programs created for ungrateful people.

If the government's books under Reagan had been subjected to the same scrutiny routinely given those of a corporation, one wonders who would have bought a share. Perusing the "balance sheet" of "U.S.A Inc.," a Montreal business research service concluded that "the company has indeed been selling the family silver." The analysis found that the "balance sheet" had "deteriorated alarmingly in recent years" and cautioned that "the increased burden of debt inevitably will start to impact on the income side of the accounts." And it lamented that there were "no signs" that U.S.A.'s management "will take the tough measures necessary to improve the company's balance sheet position."[8]

Meanwhile, a much-publicized debate over whether Congress should have a $29 million pay raise missed the point. The legislative body had become a bloated bureaucracy costing taxpayers more than $2 billion a year to maintain. This was 81 percent higher than when Reagan took office. The rise reflected a swelling payroll of some 37,500 congressional employees, plus expenses entailed in running twenty committees and eighty-seven subcommittees in the Senate and twenty-eight committees and 160 subcommittees in the House. The Senate's sergeant-at-arms managed to make eight trips to his native Hawaii between December 1987 and August 1988. Washington was setting a poor example for a nation that needed to economize.

. . .

T H E private sector was no less profligate. Few executives would deny that excessive debt is risky, but in the 1980s corporations piled up debt anyway, for the law provided benefits, at least in the near term, which seemed as far ahead as many corporate leaders wished to focus.

As debt soared at one company after another, so of course did interest charges. But unlike dividends paid on stocks, interest paid on bonds and other debt securities was tax-deductible. How easy it was for a company to buy up its outstanding stock so as to reduce its dividend obligations, and to do this through issuing tax-deductible debt securities. The effect was to reduce or even erase the corporate tax bill; this is why corporate executives were willing to shell out such huge fees to the lawyers and investment bankers helping to engineer such deals. In one typical equity-into-debt restructuring, CNW Corp., the owner of the Chicago & North Western Railroad, managed to erase entirely some $33 million in potential tax obligations, while increasing its long-term debt by nearly $800 million and its annual interest expenses by more than $110 million. Taxes paid by corporations consistently fell short of Treasury Department expectations in the late 1980s—by $20.9 billion in 1987, by $22.7 billion in 1988, and by $25 billion in 1989.

Such tactics as the CNW restructuring deepened the federal deficit and shifted more of the tax burden from corporations to families and individuals. And just as Washington disregarded the risk of a severe recession, so did corporate heads ignore the danger—though most of them had to know that it was the inevitability of a recession sooner or later that made excessive corporate debt so hazardous. Early in 1990, Texas Senator Lloyd Bentsen declared, "We've got a mystery on our hands: Well over $100 billion appears to be missing from the federal government's revenues, and we need to find out what the culprit is." Robert S. McIntyre, the director of Citizens for Tax Justice, a research group supported by organized labor, was quick to respond to Bentsen's question. "Corporations," he said, "are sending their profits to bondholders, rather than paying dividends to shareholders and taxes to the Treasury."

Zero-coupon junk bonds and pay-in-kind junk bonds were especially risky. With zero-coupon junk bonds, sometimes called superjunk, the issuers routinely assumed far more debt than they could possibly service. In one such deal, for example, Federated Department Stores issued bonds on which it theoretically paid yearly interest of 17.75 percent, entered appropriate debits on its books, and took the deductions, as the tax law permitted. But the actual payment of this interest was not scheduled to begin until 1994. Issuers of equally questionable pay-in-kind bonds were allowed to retain the right to pay interest not in cash but with more of the same dubious securities.

Who, one might ask, would buy such stuff? The disquieting answer is that by the late 1980s over 90 percent of all junk bonds were bought by institutional investors, chiefly mutual funds, banks, and insurance firms. In 1989, a research team at Columbia Law School examined the bond portfolios of two mutual funds, each with more than $1 billion in assets. Of thirty corporate issues held in one or both of the funds, seventeen had failed to earn profits equal to their interest costs, an unsustainable situation. For example, Texas Air, Southland, Western Union, and Burlington Holdings all earned at least 30 percent less than their interest costs.

"Very simply, much of the junk bond market is driven by the appearance of earnings, rather than the substance," declared Louis Lowenstein, the Columbia law professor in charge of the study. He added, "In the mutual fund literature that I have read, it is rare to find even a hint that many of these bonds are not earning their coupons, or that others pay zero in cash, or that some of those well-known companies have hollowed-out balance sheets."

The attitude of many corporate executives in the late 1980s was typified by William Farley, head of a debt-ridden underwear manufacturer called Fruit of the Loom, who praised Reagan for realizing, unlike his predecessors in the White House, that America actually was "underleveraged" and that for the government and businesses to pile up debt was good for the economy.

Under executives like Farley, American corporations assumed so much new debt in the 1980s that the share of corporate income consumed by interest costs rose from about 25 percent to nearly 50 percent. Measured against national output, corporate debt came to about 40 percent when Reagan left office, up from 30 percent in 1980. In 1988 alone, U.S. corporations spent $122.5 billion on interest payments, a record, even though interest rates had been edging down. Meanwhile, the volume of corporate bonds outstanding more than doubled, to nearly $1 trillion.

In 1988, two Princeton economists concluded that more than 10 percent of the nation's major public corporations would fail in the event of a recession comparable to the sixteen-month slump of 1973–75. They saw a possibility, in fact, that "financial stress [among corporations] would reach unprecedented levels" after Reagan.[9]

Over the course of Reagan's presidency, the median credit rating assigned to corporate bonds by Standard & Poor's slumped from A, signifying investment grade, to BB, meaning the issue was speculative and not of investment caliber. Meanwhile, corporate debt rose from about a third of the gross national product to 42 percent as corporate interest payments approached a third of cash flow—profits plus depreciation allowances. This was triple the rate prevailing only two decades earlier.

Leveraged buyouts made matters worse. Often, most of the funds raised come through the sale of junk bonds. In 1988, the volume of leveraged buyouts reached a record $67 billion, up from $3 billion in 1981. USG Corp., which was formed as Montgomery Ward in 1901, was a part of the trend. Through much of its long, proud history, the company was run by Sewell L. Avery, who abhorred debt. The firm never reported a loss nor borrowed a nickel, and it paid dividends right through the Great Depression. But in 1988, threatened by a hostile takeover by Desert Partners of Midland, Texas, USG plunged deeply into debt, borrowing $800 million to raise its total debt to $3.1 billion. In the first quarter of 1989, USG reported the first loss in its history. Struggling with huge interest payments, it laid off five hundred workers and slashed its capital outlays.

In the same quarter, as Bush entered the White House, an opportunity arose for Washington to reassert its leadership and set a standard for financial probity in private businesses. This was the report of the National Economic Commission, a bipartisan blue-ribbon panel appointed during Reagan's second term to come up with ways to limit the budget deficit. But the report, issued March 1, 1989, was deeply compromised. It offered only such politically safe generalities as the claim that "the deficit can be resolved through restraints on the growth of federal spending without increasing taxes and we recommend restraining spending increases while keeping growth strong."

As the leveraged buyouts continued, there also was no evidence of renewed, serious antitrust enforcement. The Justice Department's "antitrust division is a shadow of its former self," declared William Proxmire shortly after retiring in 1989 from thirty-one years as a Wisconsin senator. "At a time of unparalleled mergers, its staff has been cut in half, and the mighty financial interests are winning." In fact, the antitrust division did come to life in Bush's early months, but not against the array of corporate takeovers. Rather, the target was the campus, where, in the division's view, such universities as Harvard, Chicago, Wesleyan, and Amherst were unfairly restraining trade in setting similar levels of financial aid and tuition. "What's going to be next in the antitrust net?" Proxmire asked. "The Salvation Army?"

W H I L E the leveraging mounted, productivity and investment—the economy's underpinnings—stagnated. In the last two years of Reagan's presidency, hourly output in the economy's private sector rose only about 1 percent annually, while hourly compensation increased 3.8 percent in 1987 and 4.7 percent in 1988. The result, rather than increased buying power, was an accelerating rise in unit labor costs and, in turn, in inflation generally. There followed the decline, noted earlier, in what the average paycheck could purchase. As Reagan's final year wound down, the situation went from bad to worse. In the fourth quarter, productivity actually fell slightly—at an annual rate of 0.2 percent—while unit labor costs rose at a rate of 5.4 percent.

International comparisons show, moreover, that the U.S. productivity record was the sorriest among major industrial nations. While productivity stagnated in the United States, it advanced at an accelerating rate, for instance, in Japan—up 3.4 percent in 1987 and up 4.1 percent in 1988. At the same time, labor costs in Japan remained flat and purchasing power increased briskly, even before one takes account of the yen's swiftly climbing international value in Reagan's second term. The Japanese work week, it should be added, was some five hours longer than that in America, and the amount of work time lost in labor disputes in Japan came to less than 5 percent of the U.S. total. Japan also employed some 116,000 industrial robots, nearly five times as many as were employed in the much larger U.S. economy. Nor was the Japanese position unique. The typical South Korean employee worked seventeen hours longer each week than his American counterpart and the typical Taiwanese twelve hours longer. Indeed, the work week of the average American employee was appreciably shorter than those of most foreign workers, according to a 1988 survey of fifty-two cities by the Union Bank of Switzerland. It found that the global average was nearly three hours longer than the U.S. work week.

As the use of robots in Japan may suggest, productivity advances, whether in Japan or the United States or Timbuktu, depend largely on the quality of equipment available. The popular notion, of course, is that productivity gains are achieved mainly by employees rolling up their sleeves and working harder. Such efforts can make a difference. But the difference tends to be minimal, for the key lies elsewhere: in the machinery installed and in the manner in which the entire production process is arranged.

What matters is investment. In the 1980s, U.S. investment in new plant and equipment amounted to only 2.1 percent of gross national product, the lowest rate ever recorded over so long a period. The comparable readings were 3.2 percent in the decade 1971–80, as high as 3.5 percent in 1961–70, which spanned the longest economic upswing in the nation's history, and 3 percent in 1951–60. Near the end of Reagan's tenure, the average age of America's industrial base was seventeen years, compared with only ten years in Japan. Even so, only about 20 cents of every investment dollar went toward the expansion of facilities; most of the rest was spent simply to keep up existing facilities. In the period 1950–80, in contrast, 30 cents of every investment dollar was for expansion. A comparison of quality between U.S. and Japanese products is instructive. A 1987 study by the Pentagon, for instance, found a defect rate of 8 percent to 10 percent in the U.S. electronics industry, against a rate of 0.5 percent to 1 percent in the Japanese electronics industry. The difference, according to the study, was that greater attention to detail was paid at every stage of the manufacturing process in Japan.

The most important investment spending is devoted to research and development, and here too the United States lags behind. When Reagan left office, the National Science Foundation surveyed two hundred large companies that together accounted for nearly 90 percent of industrial R&D in the United States and found twenty-four of them had recently been involved in some sort of takeover scheme. The study further found that the twenty-four experienced a combined decline of 5.3 percent in their R&D spending between 1986 and 1987, while the other companies showed a modest R&D rise. Overall, company-funded R&D remained flat, or declined slightly if inflation is taken into account.

The scarcity of savings during the Reagan presidency underlies the failure to invest in productivity. Savings are crucial to investing; you can't have one without the other. To be invested, money must be saved. In his economics textbook, Paul A. Samuelson, the Nobel-laureate professor at the Massachusetts Institute of Technology, calls savings and investment "the same things."[10]

The crucial role of savings was underscored in April 1989, for instance, when Perkin-Elmer Corp., a U.S. firm that pioneered the making of advanced semiconductor chips in the early 1970s, announced that it was planning to withdraw from that business on account of overwhelming competition from a far more productive, efficient Japanese chip industry. Discussing reasons for the action, Dr. Robert Noyce, the chairman of Sematech, a government-and-industry organization set up to foster a more competitive U.S. chip industry, remarked that "it is the continued saga that there is investment money available in Japan and not in America." And, he added, "with the dismal savings rate we have, much of the American manufacturing base is being destroyed, and it doesn't bode well for the future." The American share of chip fabrication equipment, which etches circuits on silicon wafers, fell to 45 percent in 1987, down from 62 percent five years earlier. Japan's market share, by comparison, climbed to 44 percent from 29 percent in the same period.[11]

. . .

I N   the 1980s, U.S. savings, as a percentage of after-tax income, fell to the lowest levels since the 1930s. At 7.5 percent when Reagan assumed the presidency, the saving rate progressively diminished—to 6.8 percent in 1982 and on down to rates of less than 4 percent in 1987 and 1988. In some of Reagan's final months, in fact, the rate edged below 3 percent, a level not seen since 1939. In 1933, at the pit of the Great Depression, the savings rate was at an all-time low of *minus* 3.6 percent; in other words, no money was saved at all on balance and, struggling to subsist and having to liquidate assets for necessities, Americans paid out more than they took in. Private investment was also a negative number that year—minus $6.1 billion. For perspective, the savings rate in Japan in Reagan's last years exceeded 20 percent of income, more than five times the comparable U.S. rate, and the rate was rising.

While savings at the consumer level eroded sharply under Reagan, savings at the governmental level were nonexistent on account of the huge, perennial deficits in the federal budget. This governmental dissaving, as economists call it, absorbed nearly 20 cents of every dollar of private funds available for investment.[12] To balance the books, the United States was compelled to rely heavily on savings from abroad. In 1987, for example, foreigners supplied 22.5 cents of every dollar of private investment in the United States, or half again as much as American households provided. Foreigners also supplied a rising percentage of the equipment involved in this investment. As a share of this spending, imports rose to more than 42 percent at the end of Reagan's presidency from less than 30 percent three years earlier.

Why were savings so depressed? A short answer is that Americans were on a spending spree in the 1980s. Demographic trends made matters worse. In the Reagan years, a relatively large part of the population fell within the twenty-five-to-forty-four-year-old age range, and this group traditionally tends to spend an extra-large share of income. In 1981, the twenty-five-to-forty-four-year-olds constituted about 27 percent of the population, up from 23 percent a decade earlier. During the 1980s, this percentage reached a high of 32 percent in 1988. In the same period, there was also a marked rise in the share of households in the United

States represented by only one person. At 17 percent in the early 1970s, this rate reached a record 25 percent by the end of Reagan's second term. And, like the twenty-five-to-forty-four-year-old group, single-person households typically spend a relatively high portion of their earnings, partly because there is no second earner with whom to split expenses. The average person living alone in 1985 actually spent more than he or she earned, producing a negative saving rate of 2.9 percent. By comparison, the average saving rate was 3.4 percent for two-person households, 5.1 percent for three persons, and 4.2 percent for four persons.[13]

The tax laws also encouraged spending. Unlike demographics, tax regulations can be sharply altered by political leaders, but the major changes in the Reagan years only exacerbated America's extravagance. Whatever the virtues may have been, the Reagan income-tax cuts of the early 1980s, and particularly the so-called Tax Reform Act of 1986, acted to spur consumption while further reducing incentives to save.

Supply-side economic theorists had hoped that families benefiting from the tax-rate cuts would save at least part of any funds from the reductions; this promise played a key role in promoting the Reagan rate cuts. But savings fell in the wake of the 1986 act, and it became apparent that any money gained from the lowered tax rates was being spent, not saved. Increased state and local taxes also siphoned off much potential savings. The new tax regulations, moreover, included provisions distinctly hostile to saving and investing. One amounted to a steep boost in the tax rate on capital gains and another removed the investment tax credit for businesses seeking to expand and modernize their facilities. The 1986 tax act also discouraged savers by sharply curtailing eligibility for tax-sheltered individual retirement accounts, or IRAs, placed new limits on contributions to so-called 401(k) employee retirement plans as well as on corporate pension plans, and imposed a new tax on retirement benefits above certain levels. Still other new rules reduced business write-offs of depreciating assets.

In all, Reagan's tax measures, while they eliminated a number of undesirable and unfair tax-shelter loopholes, also encouraged the very patterns of overspending and undersaving that were already weakening the economy.

. . .

T H E 1986 tax cut not only discouraged saving but tended to increase the already enormous deficit in the federal budget. In the fine print of Reagan's final budget report, which he submitted in early 1989, was an estimate that the new tax rules would raise the deficit in fiscal 1990 by some $20 billion over where it would otherwise be. The 1986 act, when it was passed, was intended to be revenue-neutral, producing neither higher nor lower receipts than the regulations it supplanted. But Reagan's 1989 budget report admitted that the act had already caused a revenue loss in fiscal 1988 of $8.9 billion, and it projected further losses in fiscal 1990 of $20.3 billion, in fiscal 1991 of $16.4 billion, and in fiscal 1992 of $20.9 billion. In all, Reagan's report indicated that the new tax rules would tend to increase the national debt by more than $66 billion in four years. The losses were attributed mostly to the reduced tax rates. Revenue gains from the removal of various tax breaks, such as the investment tax credit, were supposed to offset these losses, but were not doing so.

While the connection is less than perfect, high levels of debt usually imply low savings. In the Reagan years, debt of all sorts rose steeply, not simply in absolute terms but in terms of the economy's own increasing size. Consumer debt rose 24 percent during the eight years, to 78.4 percent of gross national product, the broadest gauge of overall economic activity. Corporate debt rose 26 percent in the same period, to 32.6 percent of GNP. And the federal government's debt rose a precipitous 62 percent, to 42.4 percent of GNP.

Federal deficits, of course, require the Treasury to borrow heavily in the nation's credit markets. This, in turn, tends to push up interest rates in general and drain investment funds away from private-sector projects and toward Treasury securities, which carry a government guarantee. The effect is to deter industry's efforts to expand and modernize facilities, efforts which as we have seen are so crucial to productivity and ultimately to living standards.

The severe effect of the deficit on savings in the 1980s can be seen in what economists call net national savings—savings in the nonfederal economy, corporate as well as personal, minus the budget deficit. By and large, net national savings represent money available for investment in facilities that spur productivity—new factories, new machinery, and so on. In the 1970s, net national savings averaged 7.2 percent of the gross national product, a modestly healthy rate. But in 1988, at the end of Reagan's presidency, this rate was down to only 2.8 percent. Martin Feldstein, chief economic adviser to Reagan early in his presidency, who grew disenchanted with the administration's economic policies and eventually returned to a Harvard teaching job, argued in the closing weeks of Reagan's presidency that "reversing this decline" in savings should be "a central goal of economic policy," and stressed that the one sure path to this was "by shrinking the budget deficit." He added that "an increase in the saving rate is the key to a higher rate of economic growth," as well as to a rise in living standards. Disparaging Reagan's policies, the economist noted that "in contrast, foreign political leaders have correctly urged their citizens to save so that the resources could be devoted to investment in productivity-raising business plant and equipment, and they backed that rhetoric with tax policies designed to encourage saving."[14] When Reagan left office, the federal budget deficit in effect was absorbing some 60 percent of the nation's net savings, while the comparable rate for America's seven major trading partners was about 20 percent.

The huge federal debt reflected not only tax-cutting but federal spending, which for all the conservative talk in Washington went from record high to record high. At 22 percent of the gross national product when Reagan took office, federal outlays were close to 25 percent late in his presidency. In absolute terms, these outlays nearly doubled between 1980 and 1988, rising from less than $600 billion to $1.1 trillion. Nor did this increase reflect simply Reagan's effort to build up the military, as was commonly supposed. Outlays in the so-called entitlements area, which embraces an array of social programs, climbed 62 percent in the period, and spending for such other nondefense projects as pollution control, agriculture, and the administration of justice rose 11 percent. But the swiftest-growing budget category was interest payments to purchasers of government securities, which rose about 130 percent in the eight years.

With the federal government setting the example, debt increased apace in other sectors of the economy as well, so that total debt outstanding—governmental plus private—stood at 1.8 times the gross national product in 1988, up from 1.3 times GNP early in Reagan's tenure, as well as through most of the 1960s and 1970s. Under Reagan, the federal debt alone tripled to about $2.7 trillion. For perspective, debt merely doubled during the combined presidencies of Ford and Carter, and it took as long as thirty-one years for the first tripling of debt after World War II. The overall debt rise in the United States far outpaced comparable increases in other industrial nations. West German debt, for example, was less than 1.6 times that nation's GNP, and the ratio showed little change in the years when the U.S. ratio was surging.

C O R P O R A T E debt in the Reagan years also discouraged investment, particularly among the rising number of companies involved in leveraged takeovers and other financial restructuring schemes. Consider the leveraged buyout of the giant textile manufacturer Burlington Industries, which was taken private late in the Reagan presidency by an investor group led by Morgan Stanley & Co. A prospectus circulated at the time showed that Burlington's debt-to-equity ratio just before the deal was 0.4 to 1—that is, 40 cents of debt on Burlington's books for each $1 of equity. After the buyout, the prospectus disclosed, Burlington's debt-to-equity ratio stood at 29 to 1, or $29 of debt, much of it in so-called junk bonds carrying very high interest rates, for each $1 of equity. The report cautioned would-be investors that the interest costs of all this newly acquired debt were so large that in order to cover them, the company had to sell off substantial assets and also would require, for these asset sales to be successful, an economic environment in which general business activity was expanding at a reasonably healthy clip for a prolonged period. Deep in the report were various new restrictions on the company's future activities, imposed in part as a result of its vast new debt. Among these was one limiting the amounts that Burlington could spend on investment in new plant and equipment in future years to a fraction of what it spent before the buyout. The impact of such debt-laden deals on investment and productivity has cut across many industries, surveys show. The pattern that emerges again and again is one of lagging investment and productivity in the wake of a debt-financed restructuring in which a handful of investment banks and Wall Street lawyers enrich themselves. Struggling to raise $6.8 billion to service its huge debt, RJR Nabisco was compelled in mid-1990 to slash its capital spending 45 percent below the amount planned for the year. In 1989, the firm spent $522 million on plants and equipment, down sharply from a planned outlay of $868 million, and in the first five months of 1990, such spending came to $119 million.

With no governmental effort to discourage such deals as the Burlington buyout—not to mention such vastly larger ones as the $25 billion leveraged buyout of RJR Nabisco late in Reagan's last year—corporate debt rose even faster than federal debt. From about 80 percent of corporate financial assets when Reagan took office, corporate debt rose to 105 percent eight years later. When Bush replaced Reagan, corporate debt totaled $1.7 trillion and was rising at an annual rate of about 24 percent, a far swifter gain than for debt in any other sector of the economy.

Consumer debt rose by only about 9 percent. But in absolute terms, the consumer debt load had become huge—nearly $4 trillion, or close to the combined totals of corporate and federal debt. And in a credit-card environment in which spending and borrowing took precedence over saving and investing, millions of consumers had become as debt-ridden as Burlington or RJR Nabisco or for that matter the federal government itself, which could at least print new money to pay its bills. U.S. consumer debt was also enormous compared to that of key nations abroad. In terms of GNP, consumer debt was six times as large in the United States as in West Germany, for instance, and the U.S. total was growing nearly twice as rapidly.

Delinquent consumer debt reached $88.7 billion in 1988, more than twice the total six years earlier. About $56 billion of this was traced to uncollected income taxes, according to an analysis of the Office of Management and Budget, and much of the rest reflected delinquent loans to farmers, students, and veterans. Some 140,000 employees of the federal government itself were found to owe some $500 million. Moreover, the delinquency rate on home-mortgage loans, which normally falls when the economy is expanding and rises only in recessions, climbed sharply through the

Reagan presidency and, despite the supposed prosperity of the time, was at a record high when he left office. Especially ominous was a new slippage in the net worth of one-to-four-family homes. By early 1989, this measure of family wherewithal stood at $2,169 billion, in terms of the dollar's 1982 buying power; this was down from $2,296 billion a year earlier and from $2,307 billion in 1987. Household balance sheets were beginning to seem more in keeping with recessionary times than an economic expansion.

So consumers in general were in little better position than corporations or the federal government to furnish funds for the investments that the nation so urgently needed in order to regain its competitive edge and to reverse the incipient erosion of a once rising living standard.

U N D E R Reagan, too many priorities were out of whack. The national mood, which Reagan had encouraged, demanded fast gratification, and there was little thought of the longer run. It was as if the whole country were on cocaine in one form or another.

A reflection of this mood was the electorate's propensity to split the ballot, voting in national contests for candidates deemed, however mistakenly, to be relatively frugal, but in home-turf contests for candidates known to spend freely. A Republican in the White House who at least paid lip service to fiscal restraint served to ease among voters the fear that they might have to consume less. And a free-spending Democrat in Congress ensured that Uncle Sam would in fact continue to press projects that brought federal largess. In 1988, for example, 135 congressional districts went for George Bush, a conservative Republican, over Michael Dukakis, a liberal Democrat, and yet opted for Democrats for the House of Representatives. By comparison, only thirteen districts went the other way, voting for Dukakis over Bush for president, and for a Republican for the House. Many of these Republicans hardly advocated belt-tightening. An example was Bill Green of the 15th congressional district in Manhattan. First elected in 1978, Green won easily in 1988, even though Dukakis collected 66 percent of the liberal-leaning district's presidential ballots. Dukakis's appeal in the 15th district, which years ago sent John Lindsay, then a Republican, to Washington, was in large measure his liberalism. But this was Green's appeal as well. He was the congressman who, voters in the district believed, would bring home the most pork. His views on most spending issues were closer to those of Dukakis than those of Bush, who headed the party's ticket.

The energy issue reflected a similar attitude. Less than a decade earlier, during the Arab oil squeeze, Americans were forced to wait in line at the gasoline pump and even to drive less. During the Reagan years, however, this warning that the nation must grow more self-reliant and less wasteful in the energy area was largely dismissed. According to the Department of Energy, the United States in 1989 was using 20.1 British thermal units to produce $1 worth of goods and services, which was appreciably less than in the early 1970s before the oil squeeze. But the total had been edging up since 1985. In 1988, the U.S. consumed about six-tenths of a ton of oil for each $1,000 of goods and services, compared to only three-tenths of a ton for Japan and four-tenths for major industrial nations as a whole.

In the 1988 presidential campaign, energy was a nonissue. At the time, Frank G. Zarb, the federal energy administrator during the oil squeeze, remarked that this voter "complacency has occurred even as evidence suggests that the country is on the verge of losing whatever time was bought a decade ago" through measures to spur oil conservation. In the last five years of Reagan's presidency, oil consumption in the U.S. rose 10 percent, while oil imports jumped 40 percent and domestic output fell 5 percent. Moreover, the search for other forms of energy came, as Zarb put it, "to a virtual standstill." Zarb recognized that "what needs to be done is historically unpopular"—steps to discourage the use of oil, especially from abroad. But a special tax on gasoline was opposed by 73 percent of the public, according to a nationwide poll.[15]

At about the same time, a group of leading scientists estimated that at the consumption rates then prevailing, the world had less than fifty years of oil supply left. But in 1988 such considerations were far from the minds of most Americans, either in Washington or on Main Street, and the Iraqi invasion of Kuwait was two years in the future.

Another sign of shortsightedness was that while poverty rates were rising for children, they were falling for the elderly. Spending for Social Security and Medicare together came to nearly 7 percent of the gross national product in 1988, up from less than 3 percent a couple of decades earlier, while all other federal spending edged down slightly in terms of GNP. By the end of Reagan's presidency, poverty was less prevalent among the elderly than among any other age group in the population. It would stretch the point, perhaps, to say that improved conditions among old people were achieved directly at the expense of the young. But the lobbying power of the elderly was vastly greater than that of the young, and therefore it is no surprise that Washington was far more charitable toward the old. Yet, on the campaign trail in 1988, Bush declared that the "national character can be measured in how we care for our children" and Dukakis hailed the young as "our joy and our future."

In fact, some forty thousand American babies died that year as a result of inadequate prenatal care. This was the worst infant-death rate among nineteen industrial nations, and, according to the Urban Institute, the nation's childhood poverty rate was two to three times higher than in the other nations. In 1988, federal outlays totaled $4 billion for child nutrition and $11 billion for family support programs, and means tests were required in each instance. By comparison, the corresponding outlays came to $86 billion for Medicare and $217 billion for Social Security, and no means testing was required.[16]

In all, more than 40 percent of the federal budget was devoted to the elderly. When Reagan left the White House, the typical senior citizen in America had never been better off. Six of every ten people over sixty-five had fully paid-off home mortgages, and the age group as a whole, though it made up only 11 percent of the population, held title to about 30 percent of all tangible assets and 40 percent of all financial assets. The group's poverty rate was 12 percent, down from 25 percent in the 1970s, and its average income was higher than that of adults in their twenties. Outfits that work hard in Washington to ensure continued federal largess for the elderly include such powerful organizations as the American Association of Retired Persons, the National Association of Retired Federal Employees, and the American Legion.

But again, priorities needed reordering when Bush took office.

Expanding steadily near the close of Reagan's presidency, the economy's nonprofit sector comprised some 925,000 organizations, ranging from the most prestigious universities and hospitals to the YMCA. This was roughly triple the number of nonprofits only two decades earlier. In the same period, by comparison, the number of for-profit companies merely doubled, to about three million. In the same two decades, moreover, the number of applications for nonprofit status received each year by the Internal Revenue Service rose to nearly 64,000 from about 14,000.

A flourishing nonprofit organization in the 1980s was the National Bureau of Economic Research. Based in Cambridge, Massachusetts, the academically oriented NBER drew much of its financial support from corporations and wealthy individuals, for whom the contributions represented a deductible expense. Occasionally, NBER research was useful, but often the topics seemed merely a waste of funds supplied ultimately at taxpayer expense. My favorite example of this waste, since I happen to enjoy an occasional game of golf, was an NBER analysis in June 1988. Titled "Do Tournaments Have Incentive Effects?" the forty-five-page study, which was replete with complex formulas, charts, and tables, explored whether "the level and structure of prizes" in professional golf tournaments "influence players' performance." The conclusion, not surprisingly, was that "higher prize levels do lead, *ceteris paribus,* to lower scores."

Congress legislates the kinds of institutions that may qualify for tax-exempt and tax-deductible status, and the IRS decides whether a particular organization qualifies. As the number of applications granted rose, so naturally did the amount of potential revenue lost to the government. Early in Reagan's presidency, this loss was put at $9.7 billion yearly, and the sum was estimated to have swelled to nearly $20 billion by the time Bush was in the White House.[17]

This meant that taxpayers, from large corporations to individual wage earners, shouldered more and more of the tax burden. The fast-rising nonprofits also posed unfair competition. When Bush became president, the nonprofits were taking in about $300 billion annually, of which some $15 billion was from earnings and fees for goods and services offered in direct competition with for-profit enterprises. An example was the National Capital Center YMCA in Washington. A full membership to its plush "athletic center" cost slightly over $1,000, a hard-to-match package for the well-heeled area's competing taxpaying health clubs. Legislative relief for the clubs was unlikely, since the center's members included, among other influential people, many congressional representatives and their families.[18]

Altruism of another sort, concern for the unborn, was evident in the drive, which Reagan enthusiastically endorsed, to ban abortion. The Republican party's 1988 campaign platform put it this way: "The unborn child has a fundamental right to live which cannot be infringed." However admirable such sentiments may appear, they neatly overlook their eventual cost. Lloyd N. Cutler, the White House counsel in the Carter administration, has noted, "The same voters and legislators who would force the mother to bear her child have done precious little to provide for the health and welfare of the 1.2 million teenage mothers who, for one reason or another, did not choose to abort their pregnancies." And in their pro-life zeal, he has warned, the anti-abortionists forget that "for every unwanted child they force into the world, they may be piling huge obligations on all of us that our government would be bound to satisfy."[19] The upshot was yet another burden down the road for an economy already strained by surging transfer payments and insufficient tax revenues.

Working its way through Congress, meanwhile, was the proposed Americans with Disabilities Act, mandating, among other things, that all new buses be made "fully accessible" to handicapped riders. Requiring wheelchair lifts and ramps, as well as wider on-board restrooms and aisles, the plan was estimated to increase the costs of each new bus, on the average, by from $15,000 to as much as $50,000. For all the proposal's good intentions, the costs involved—to be borne by bus operators—threatened eventually to cripple the bus industry. Not all bus companies would fail, according to Wayne J. Smith, executive director of the United Bus Owners of America, but the few surviving lines that charged enough to stay in business would be priced out of the range of the primary bus riders—mainly low-income families, senior citizens, students, and people afraid or unable to fly, or whose trips are to rural locations far from any airport.

About the same time, Washington launched a program to pay

the city's high school students $3.35 an hour simply to attend summer classes. Called the Merit Scholar Training Program, the plan managed to attract sixty teenagers who met with school-system teachers every weekday for five hours of drill in math and verbal skills. Washington officials hoped through the program to improve the city's poor showing in such academic competitions as the National Merit Scholarships. Such a goal may be admirable, but this cannot be said for a policy of doling out funds to persuade students to attend classes designed to help them. The program was hardly designed to instill initiative and, in any event, was launched at a time of deepening financial distress for the city's economy.

While Washington's teenagers were being bribed with tax-payer funds to attend school, Congress was voting to lop $45,000 from an annual federal endowment for the arts totaling $171 million. This slim cutback, however, had nothing to do with saving money. Rather, it was prompted by congressional dismay at the sort of art that the federal money was underwriting, such as *Piss Christ,* which was a plastic crucifix submerged in the artist's urine, and several photographs depicting sadomasochistic homosexual encounters.

Meanwhile, the political rhetoric in Washington showed little recognition of any limits on economic resources or any need for rationing choices. Only a half year into his new presidency, Bush used the twentieth anniversary of man's first moon landing to urge "a sustained program of manned exploration of the solar system—and yes, the permanent settlement of space," including a manned mission to Mars and, within a decade, a manned space station. The estimated price tag was put at about $400 billion, but Bush said nothing about how such a sum was to be raised.

This proposal repeated a pattern that "is part of the Reagan legacy," declared the chairman of the House Budget Committee at the time, Leon E. Panetta, a California Democrat. "You do a press release, you do your PR on a new program or a new endeavor, and you do the hype that day . . . and then you walk away from it. You don't say how you're going to pay for it." The aim, Panetta said, was to create "an image of a rich bounty of funds" when nothing of the sort in fact existed. Such tactics, it should be noted, extended to many areas. The new administration proudly talked of $441 million more for education, but "there simply wasn't anything more," according to an official of the American Council of Education. Along a similar line were unrealistic promises of hefty foreign aid, especially to East European countries. Panetta feared that Bush was "in danger of becoming a classic example of an overpromising politician . . . the Babe Ruth of promises, but when it comes to telling us how he is going to pay for all these promises, he's Casey at the bat, unable to deliver the crucial funds."[20]

The price tag on Bush's promises, by Panetta's estimate, included $70 billion for the B-2 bomber, $69 billion for the Star Wars missile defense system, $6 billion for a superconducting supercollider used in nuclear research, $2.4 billion for a year's fight against drugs and crime, $150 billion, at a minimum, in federal bailout costs for the savings-and-loan industry, and another $150 billion, at the least, to clean up nuclear weapons plants—not to mention such relatively trifling sums as $145 million in economic aid to Poland and Hungary.

"The issue is leadership," Panetta declared, urging Bush to level with the American people by facing up openly to the "tough choices facing us." It was not, the congressman added, "too late to change course."

CHAPTER FOUR

━━━━━━━━

HARD TIMES

Americans did not fight and win the wars of the twentieth century to make the world safe for green vegetables. If we were to regulate houses with the same principles we now apply to our food and air, for example, we would all have to live in single-story homes—for fear of falling down stairs.
—Richard G. Darman, Bush's budget director, in a speech at
Harvard University on May 1, 1990

A S T H E 1990s began, debt was continuing to pile up, albeit more slowly, at corporations and in households. Worrisome at any time, such trends were especially unsettling in an economic expansion about to complete its eighth year in November 1990.

In the past, after so long a period of broad economic growth and accumulation, corporate and family finances were usually strong. But after a decade of junk-bond financing, U.S. corporations had retired nearly $500 billion in equity and taken on nearly $1 trillion in debt, so their interest payments now consumed over a third of their cash flow, more than at the worst point of any recent recession. Time Warner Inc. reported a first-quarter 1990 loss of $51 million and blamed it on interest costs stemming from Time's recent acquisition of Warner Communications. RJR Nabisco, Inc., reported a $222 million loss for the same quarter, and again the reason was the expense of servicing massive new debt, in this instance from the leveraged buyout of RJR by Kohlberg Kravis Roberts & Co. in 1989.

New policies were sorely needed to set the economy on a

sound course and deal with the festering problems left by excesses of the 1980s. But the government, overextended on all
fronts, was ill-equipped to fight the inevitable, if long postponed,
downturn in the business cycle. Bush was still the nice guy riding
high in popularity polls and was reluctant to undertake a risky
change of course, nor was it clear what a better course would be.
So the problems grew.

America's net foreign debt was close to $670 billion at the start
of 1990, up from only $10 billion as recently as 1984. And the
federal budget deficit in March 1990 rose to a record $53.34 bil-
lion, eclipsing the previous monthly record of $39.4 billion set in
May 1986. The showing would have been even worse were Social
Security payroll taxes not still financing the government's current
operations, which masked the true deficit. Even with the gimmickry, the reported deficit was $151.7 billion for the first eight
months of fiscal 1990, up from $113.2 billion in the same 1989
period. For 1990, interest payments on the national debt would
exceed $180 billion and the debt itself would exceed $10,000 per
individual, more than $40,000 per family of four. It was rising at
a rate of more than $900,000 a minute.

With all of this, the Bush administration continued to gloss
over the situation, projecting a deficit of only $121 billion for the
entire fiscal year, an impossibility. As the costs of the S&L bailout
kept mounting, a likelier deficit figure was more than $200 bil-
lion—or more than $300 billion without the use of smoke and
mirrors, such as excluding costs of the S&L bailout and "borrowing" from a Social Security surplus supposedly set aside for the
eventual retirement of the baby-boom generation. Predictably, an
amendment was working its way through Congress to change the
rules of Gramm-Rudman-Hollings to exempt S&L cleanup expenses.

In mid-July—two weeks before Iraq's invasion of Kuwait
placed expected new strains on the Pentagon's budget—Bush's
Office of Management and Budget forecast a fiscal 1991 deficit of
$231.4 billion, nearly $132 billion higher than its January estimate
and nearly $168 billion over the Gramm-Rudman target for the
year. A Gallup Poll taken several days after the new forecast
found, not surprisingly, that Americans now ranked the federal
deficit in a tie with drugs as the nation's most pressing problem.

In September 1989, in a similar survey, concern about drugs was eight times greater than concern about the deficit.

Huge deficits were everywhere—not just in the federal budget and foreign trade, but in a decaying infrastructure, in inadequate health care, in a deteriorating environment. There was much wishful talk of a "peace dividend" as the Cold War ended, but no sign of one. There was a disheartening lack of leadership in Washington and a rising distrust on Main Street of the government's ability any longer to do anything right. Looking up like hungry sheep for leadership, people saw a need for action, but Bush, for all his nice-guy popularity, was inert, afraid to offend his far-right constituency, the only one he felt he could count on.

Polls showed that most Americans were willing to sacrifice for a cleaner environment. In mid-April, Bush convened an eighteen-nation conference in Washington ostensibly to seek answers to the so-called greenhouse effect. Typically, he proposed no steps, merely cautioning against "environmental policies that ignore the economic factor" and leaving the foreign delegates wondering why he had bothered to bring them together. A month later, the White House decided to withdraw its support for an international plan to assist Third World countries in the phasing out of chemicals that deplete the earth's ozone layer. The decision followed closely a speech at Harvard University in which Budget Director Richard G. Darman likened the environmental movement to "a green mask under which different faces of politico-ideology can hide." Finally, in mid-June, the White House under pressure agreed to support the plan, though it urged limiting the U.S. contribution to about $20 million, far less than the amount already authorized in Congress.

Meanwhile, Washington continued to perform as a mere reshuffler of funds, and a patently corrupt and chaotic one. From housing to the savings-and-loan bailout, scandals permeated federal programs. When, people asked, did Washington last initiate a major program that worked? The Clean Air Act of 1970? Placing a man on the moon in 1969? Initiating the Interstate Highway System in 1956? Or was it mobilizing for World War II? A startling statistic: To bail out the corrupt savings-and-loan industry would require more dollars (though of course much cheaper ones) than the $290 billion spent for World War II.

By 1990, the United States had little money or resources for the struggling new democracies in Eastern Europe—a tragic loss of opportunity. When West German Chancellor Helmut Kohl and Soviet President Gorbachev met at a Russian spa in mid-July and agreed on a German reunification plan, the Bush administration was reduced to professing that it didn't feel left out. About the same time, at a press conference of major Western powers' foreign secretaries, nearly an hour elapsed before any reporter tossed a question at James Baker, the American representative.

A disturbing new pattern in foreign trade was also eroding our opportunities. Within the overall U.S. trade deficit there had begun to appear, for the first time since the early post–World War II years, a shortfall in the once-robust services category. Dollars flowing out of the country to service mounting foreign debt had started to outnumber those flowing in from travel, entertainment, insurance, and other service items. This was ominous, since for years hefty surpluses in services had more than offset deficits in merchandise trade.

At home, signs of economic trouble were increasing. A survey found that general business activity had begun to slip in as many as thirty-four states. In particular difficulty were the more populous areas of the Northeast, such as Boston and New York City, centers closely tied to the slumping financial-services and high-technology industries in which the United States had continued to lose competitive advantage to Japan and other producers.[1] In New York City, the median price of a home had fallen in a year to $166,000 from $193,000. In Boston, the Bank of New England, saddled with worthless real-estate loans, was struggling to keep afloat through huge cash injections from the Federal Reserve.

While real-estate prices sagged, inflation worsened for consumers. In the first quarter of 1990, the consumer price index rose at an annual rate of nearly 9 percent, the sharpest increase in nearly a decade and a pace, were it to persist, that would halve the dollar's buying power in a bare eight years. Around the same time, the Tax Foundation estimated that in 1990 "tax freedom day" would occur on the latest date ever: May 5. This meant that it would take until then for the average taxpayer to earn enough to cover all tax bills—federal, including Social Security, plus state and local. As recently as 1984, the date was April 28. What had happened, people wondered, to the much-touted supply-side tax cuts?[2] A Conference Board survey in April found rising concern among workers about retirement, as more and more companies, with profits falling or nonexistent, cut back on medical and other benefits for their retirees.

In Bush's first months, many firms recently restructured through leveraged buyouts and other debt-laden maneuvers were in deep trouble. Resorts International Inc., saddled with some $915 million of long-term debt, announced a debt-service moratorium near the end of August 1989. Firms in default included the Cannon Group, Dart Drug Stores, General Homes, LTV, Maxicare Health Plans, Public Service of New Hampshire, Revco, Southmark, and Campeau's huge U.S. retailing units. Others seeking to restructure oppressive debt included Merv Griffin's Griffin Resorts, Integrated Resources, and Seaman Furniture. Investor reaction to such developments was evident when, for example, nearly $475 million of junk bonds yielding 15 percent could not be marketed for Ohio Mattress Co., the producer of such standbys as Sealy and Stearns & Foster mattresses. A few days later, two other junk-bond offerings totaling more than $1.2 billion, for Grand Union Co., the supermarket firm, and Ethan Allen & Co., the furniture retailer, were called off because investors were no longer interested.

As many corporations struggled with debt, overall spending for research and development began to fall, raising fresh concern about competitiveness. "We've moved from research and development being a corporate asset to where it's what a corporate raider looks for first [to cut] and get cash flow," remarked William J. Spencer, Xerox's executive vice president for R&D.[3] In the early 1980s, in contrast, R&D spending had risen between 6 percent and 12 percent a year.

While public dismay grew over findings of massive fraud in the collapsing S&L industry, questions were beginning to arise over the safety of such normally secure investments as money-market mutual funds, with assets in early 1990 of some $390 billion scattered through more than twenty million accounts. The worry was that commercial paper—essentially IOUs from corporations—had grown to over 50 percent of the funds' holdings, nearly twice the rate in the early 1980s, and as corporate bankruptcies increased, so did commercial-paper defaults. When Drexel Burnham Lambert entered Chapter 11, its bankruptcy filing showed over $750 million of such paper on its books, backed mainly by illiquid junk bonds.

Most troubling were signs that the leadership in Washington—within the 101st Congress as well as in the Bush White House—lacked political courage. Persisting in a long-standing game of budget gimmickry, the White House and Congress agreed, for example, to shift the military's payday, scheduled for October 2, 1989, a Monday, to September 29, 1989, a Friday and the next-to-last day of fiscal year 1989 for the federal budget, "saving" $2.9 billion in the fiscal 1990 budget. The decision around the same time to move the U.S. Postal Service off-budget produced another "saving" of some $2 billion. The Postal Service remained within the federal workmen's compensation program in case of injuries to its personnel, however, which led to yet another deception, involving the bookkeeping for its payments into that program. The payments were allowed to be counted as receipts to the Treasury, rather than simply as an intergovernmental transfer of funds. The result: another $330 million "saved."

Meanwhile, the Federal Housing Administration was under mounting strain, with more money flowing out than in, its cash dwindling, and its inventory of foreclosed homes mounting. Even so, legislators were pushing to expand rather than curtail the strapped agency's activities. Under new legislation, the FHA was now able to guarantee home-mortgage loans of up to nearly $125,000, about 25 percent more than before.

Elsewhere on the housing front, another agency in difficulty was the Department of Housing and Urban Development. Supervision at HUD had all but disappeared under its Reagan-appointed secretary, Samuel R. Pierce. In July 1989, Bush's new housing secretary, Jack F. Kemp, the former conservative congressman from New York, found that fraud and mismanagement during the Pierce regime had cost the government at least $2 billion and possibly as much as $6 billion. HUD had been "run in a slipshod manner," he said, with a pattern of "abuse and mismanagement, fraud and favoritism." He cited, for instance, a California country club where $15 million of HUD money was invested in a golf course, tennis courts, and swimming pools. He proposed ending FHA-insured mortgage loans for vacation homes and urged stricter rules to keep such loans from "real estate speculators" and "no-money-down operators." Kemp also called for an increase to $100 million in the budget for monitoring HUD programs, up from the $25 million set aside after a series of cuts under Reagan. In addition, he ordered annual audits for the FHA, which had not been subjected to one in fifteen years. HUD was intended, of course, to serve low-income people, but instead, as Kemp noted, it now "was serving upper- and middle-income persons, and doing it very poorly at that." In May 1990, HUD auditors reckoned that the government faced a bill of $177 billion for defaulted loans to projects involving golf courses, tennis courts, and marinas. One $15.4 million project in Niceville, Florida, included tennis courts, twenty-seven holes of golf, a large swimming pool, and a marina with 120 boat slips. Moreover, it was approved in April 1989, two months after Kemp took charge of HUD, in violation of agency rules against resort-type projects.

Another troubled agency was the thirty-five-year-old Small Business Administration. A favorite of the Reagan White House, the agency's annual budget had recently been reduced, with its loan-guarantee program to fledgling enterprises cut by a fifth to $2.4 billion and its direct-loan program slashed by three quarters to $90 million. But in 1989, funding for the SBA began to expand again, a response to small-business lobbying and such congressmen as John LaFalce, the New York Democrat heading the House's Small Business Committee, who declared, "I will not only fight any attempts to dismantle SBA, I intend to fight for increases in SBA programs, which not only benefit small businesses but also our economy." In 1988, the agency ran a deficit of nearly $9 billion, yet its benefits were bestowed on only about 2 percent of the thirteen million small businesses then in operation, and it employed 4,600 people to process thirty thousand loans.

Health care was also a mounting problem that Bush seemed reluctant to face. In February 1990, the National Bureau of Economic Research estimated that with existing trends, health-care costs would absorb about 20 percent of national income within two decades. Still, neither Bush nor congressional leaders would deal seriously with the prospect. Even small, relatively painless steps were deemed too large to be attempted. The University of Michigan's School of Public Health estimated that doubling the cigarette tax would cut the population of teenage smokers by close to 20 percent—and improve long-term health prospects for some 800,000 young people. But to enact this proposal required the courage to deal with the tobacco lobby. Bush was similarly averse to endorsing such sensible but controversial proposals as to let elderly people die who were desperately ill and were being kept alive at great expense against their will.

Late in 1989, Congress repealed an effort to inject more fiscal responsibility into so-called catastrophic health care by assessing the elderly, who of course would benefit, for the expense of broadened coverage. In 1988, Congress had enlarged Medicare to cover hospital stays, nursing-home care, and drug costs, and to pay for this it had imposed new taxes, charging all 33 million Medicare recipients a flat fee. Also, up to 50 percent of the wealthiest Medicare recipients would pay a new surtax, which by 1993 would reach a ceiling of $2,100 per couple. But after lobbyists attacked the plan, the legislators retreated, repealing legislation that then-President Reagan had hailed as "historic." The seniors' lobbying, according to Senator John D. Rockefeller IV of West Virginia, left "people on the Hill really shell-shocked." Dan Rostenkowski, the Democratic chairman of the House Ways and Means Committee, lamented the "uneven contest" for federal support between old and young Americans, adding that "the old have gotten more while the young have gotten less."

With strong leadership from Bush this might not have happened; he could have urged—but did not—that elderly people in middle- and upper-income brackets be made responsible for more of their medical expenses, particularly routine costs. He also could have encouraged—but did not—increased consumer choice in health care as a way to curb the costs by rewarding cost-conscious individuals. To no avail, the Heritage Foundation proposed eliminating all tax exclusions for employer-provided health insurance. Under the proposal, individuals would get direct tax relief for medical or health-insurance expenses, and people careful in selecting their medical care and insurance plans would get to keep any money saved, whereas under the existing system such savings went back to employers.[4]

Doctors' fees under Medicare were widely recognized as a major factor in the rapidly rising cost of health care. In November 1989, a congressional commission made up of doctors and economists proposed a long list of fee reductions. It suggested, for example, that the charge for hip-replacement surgery be cut to $1,985 from $2,404; for a coronary-artery bypass, to $2,828 from $3,894; for a partial colon removal, to $1,072 from $1,256; for a cataract removal and lens insert, to $1,164 from $1,467; for an electrocardiogram, to $25 from $35; and for a chest X-ray, to $10 from $12. To protect patients from charges far above the Medicare rates, doctors would be allowed, starting in 1992, to charge no more than 25 percent over the Medicare ceilings, and this would later be cut to 15 percent. But without strong White House support, the plan languished. In the 1980s, it should be noted, physicians' incomes rose about 8 percent a year, on the average, nearly twice the average annual gain of about 5 percent for workers generally.

Headway against illegal drug use would of course help ease the health-care burden, as well as reduce crime. In 1988 alone, some $2.5 billion was spent just to care for babies of crack-addicted mothers. To prepare such infants only for kindergarten was costing an estimated $15 billion yearly. And this did not include the later, additional expense of special learning programs in higher grades, which has been put as high as $12 billion a year. For all Bush's campaign talk about waging a "war on drugs" and stopping "this scourge," he seemed unwilling to meet the problem head-on through improved treatment facilities and drug education—measures deemed essential by virtually all substance-abuse experts. Instead, there were increasing calls to legalize cocaine and heroin, much as alcohol was legalized after prohibition; a typical advocate was Milton Friedman, the free-market economist and longtime adviser to Republican presidents.

To their credit, Bush and William Bennett, his drug-war czar, resisted the legalization arguments, but they also were unwilling to lead the costly effort of treatment and education that the problem demanded, with some fourteen million Americans paying roughly $100 billion a year for illicit drugs. With legalization, drug prices no doubt would drop sharply, perhaps as much as 90 percent. But the various substances would become even easier to obtain and in the end drug use would surely increase, as would the health problems associated with it.[5] Ultimately, the expense would far outweigh the near-term cost of improved treatment and education that Bush and Bennett sought to avoid.

Cleaning up and protecting the environment also required a greater effort than Bush seemed willing to make. With tighter federal regulation, the eleven-million-gallon oil spill of the Exxon Valdez in Alaska in 1989 might never have occurred. Rules were disregarded not only aboard ship but at facilities ashore. By mid-1990, legislation to toughen regulations and reduce the likelihood of another such spill was still bottled up in Congress, strongly opposed by the oil industry and lacking White House support.

Similarly, the Bush administration opposed legislation in 1990 that would have set significantly higher standards for air quality by mandating catalytic converters guaranteed to work for at least the average life of a car, about 100,000 miles, and the use of gasoline with a higher oxygen content, which burns more cleanly, in cities with severe smog problems. What did emerge from Congress, with Bush's blessing, was a watered-down clean-air bill that worried many environmental experts. For the United States to halve acid rain emissions in a decade would cost an estimated $700 million annually over the first five years and $3.8 billion annually in the second five. To bring all U.S. cities into compliance with air-quality standards for ozone would cost close to $4 billion a year. To eliminate three quarters of the cancer deaths caused by toxic emissions from factories would cost about $2 billion annually. But the legislation fell far short of such goals.

The administration was also reluctant to address such long-term threats as the so-called greenhouse effect, the warming of the atmosphere from pollutants, which studies show is causing, for example, the sea level to rise. In contrast, the low-lying Netherlands by 1990 had already spent more than $15 billion on coastal defenses against a rising sea level. Though the rise poses a long-term hazard for the United States as well, it was receiving little thought from the administration or from Congress, and no money. To convene fruitless multinational meetings in Washington was no help.

For Bush to take such positions was shortsighted, because the longer the delay in addressing such challenges to protect the environment, the larger the eventual cost. As Frederic Krupp, executive director of the Environmental Defense Fund, has re-marked, nations with the strictest environmental requirements "are going to be the ones best able to compete in the world marketplace" in coming decades.

N O one knows how much more than Bush's early estimates the S&L mess ultimately will cost. It was increasingly evident by mid-1990 that the bill would far exceed the Bush administration's original figure of about $160 billion. Estimates started at a mini-mum of $300 billion and ranged higher than $600 billion. In March, the House Banking Committee reported that the bailout funds proposed would fall at least $30 billion, and possibly as much as $162 billion, short of the amount required simply to deal with failing S&Ls. FIRREA, the bailout legislation, was enacted in Au-gust 1989, and provided $50 billion to close or sell failed thrift units through 1992. But all but $2 billion of that sum had been used just to cover losses already sustained at the nearly four hundred S&Ls seized by the government through early March of 1990.

For the full decade, even a bailout cost as unrealistically low as $200 billion was more than $1,300 for each taxpayer. This was more than projected federal outlays for such pressing needs as combating drugs, repairing roads, pollution control, helping the homeless, or improving preschool education. The bailout legisla-tion was based on the prospect that the government would even-tually have to take over some four hundred S&Ls at the most, but by 1990 the likelihood was that the eventual total would top eight hundred. For perspective, as recently as 1987 the Reagan admin-istration had assured Congress that cleaning up the S&L mess would cost no more than $10 billion. As the takeovers continued, by March 1990, with the seizure of the Imperial Savings and Loan Association, the government had become the holder of some $4.3 billion of junk bonds. When the budget deficit set a record in March 1990, the S&L bailout was blamed for much of it, and of course the bailout effort had barely begun. By midyear, estimates of the ultimate cost ranged above $1 trillion. A Stanford Univer-sity report placed the total at nearly $1.4 trillion over forty years. Even pollution added to the cost, since more than four hundred of the seized properties were found to contain hazardous wastes that now were the government's responsibility.

The wonder is that public anger was not greater. Among the few to raise his voice in outrage was Senator John Kerry, a Democratic member of the Senate Banking Committee. The senator warned that there would eventually be widespread public anger that so many savings-and-loan "criminals" had so successfully sheltered so much "looted" money simply by placing it in secret bank accounts abroad. And the Bush administration, he charged, was doing "very little about it." The same, of course, could be said about many senators and congressional representatives in Kerry's own party.

No doubt the degree of public outrage would have been greater early on were the bailout not so complicated an undertaking.

SAVINGS & LOAN BAILOUT COST ESTIMATES

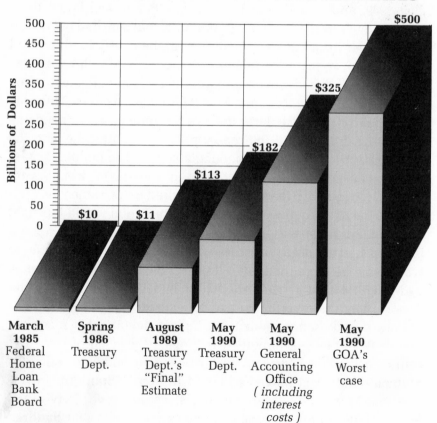

Source: Treasury Department, FDIC, GAO

Under the one-thousand-page bailout law, S&Ls were ordered to keep at least some 70 percent of their assets in mortgage-related investments, while previously there were virtually no constraints on where depositors' funds might be put. The thrift units were also required, for example, to have tangible capital—that is, the excess of their assets over their liabilities—amounting to at least 1.5 percent of their assets, with the rate rising to 3 percent by 1994. When the new law was passed, 672 S&Ls showed capital rates below 1.5 percent and another three hundred were under 3 percent. To meet this more stringent standard, as well as other similar tests, many thrifts were compelled to sell assets to increase their capital relative to assets. In August 1989, overall S&L assets fell $13.4 billion, and as rates paid to savers dropped as well, deposit withdrawals came to $5.1 billion more than the inflow.

When Bush signed the bailout legislation, efforts were already under way to beef up the S&L regulatory force. The staff of federal regulators, at 1,036 in 1984, was up to 2,120, and entry-level salaries, though still niggardly at just over $20,000, had doubled in five years. Also, training courses were stretched to fourteen days from nine. A few months later, Attorney General Richard Thornburgh announced that the Justice Department, at an added yearly cost of some $50 million, was assigning an additional four hundred prosecutors, agents, and accounting personnel to the agency's already expanded "antifraud enforcement" of the savings-and-loan industry. By early 1990, federal regulators had arranged for the sales of sixty S&Ls and assumed control over nearly four hundred units with assets totaling $193 billion. As a result of such activities, the federal government had become the largest single operator of financial institutions in the United States, moving ahead of Citibank, the previous front-runner.

Under Reagan, whose goal was to reduce regulation, federal savings-and-loan regulators relaxed their supervision but continued to guarantee deposits regardless of how risky an S&L's investments might be. In 1982, ceilings on interest rates that S&Ls could pay were blithely lifted and the thrifts were given far more latitude in their investment choices. Federal regulation, in other words, invited S&Ls to speculate wildly at the taxpayers' expense, which they did. Between 1981 and 1984, the number of federal S&L examiners was cut sharply. Yet, for all the speculating, the government remained ready to insure all deposits up to $100,000.

Typical in this deregulated-but-guaranteed environment was the behavior of CenTrust Bank, a Miami-based S&L, which plowed more than $1 billion into junk bonds, as well as $20 million into, of all things, works of pre-eighteenth-century art. In 1989, regulators ordered that the collection be assigned a book value of zero and called for the troubled institution to halt dividend payments on its preferred stock. Above $15 in 1986, CenTrust shares were selling below $3 by October 1989. As Michigan Congressman John D. Dingell put it, "Deregulation has enriched scoundrels and knaves and created an ongoing scandal that could fill the jailhouses." In the first seven months of 1989, as many as 262 S&Ls with $104 billion in assets were seized by the government. Another 250 were deemed by regulators likely soon to fail, and of 2,946 S&Ls still thought to be relatively sound, roughly a third were expected nonetheless to fail as well within a couple of years. By the start of 1990, the surviving S&Ls were losing money at a rate of $3 million an hour, on top of a record $19 billion loss for 1989 as a whole. This was nearly three times what the government had budgeted for its so-called war on drugs in 1990 and some $6 billion more than S&Ls lost in 1988.

By the spring of 1990, the government was running 330 S&Ls in thirty-nine states and had sold or liquidated another ninety-three. The number of healthy units was down to 1,273, and another 1,295 were still operating but deemed unhealthy and likely to fail. Meanwhile, L. William Seidman, chairman of the Federal Deposit Insurance Corporation and the Resolution Trust Corporation, was encountering increasing administrative difficulties. RTC was authorized to employ a staff of ten thousand, but funds were available for only fourteen hundred people. Moreover, the agency had no funds to offer financing to prospective buyers of the approximately 35,000 properties that it had taken over and was trying to sell, an effort bound to depress an already struggling real-estate industry. Worth an estimated $14.9 billion when seized, the properties would have to be discounted by huge amounts—30 percent and up—to attract buyers. The inventory included twenty-four athletic clubs, 162 golf-course resorts, fifty-one mobile-home parks, thirty-eight marinas, sixty-two ranches, sixteen garages, two uranium mines, and a coal mine. Under the frantic sales procedure, outrageously, a property holder who had defaulted could now repurchase assets at vastly lower prices. Henry B. Gonzales, the Texas Democrat chairing the House Banking Committee, declared that "President Bush's great promises are drowning in a sea of indecision, inaction, and infighting" within the bailout bureaucracy.

The tangle of overlapping responsibilities was apparent in an organizational chart produced in early 1990 for the various regulatory agencies involved in the bailout. The mindless bailout effort under Bush was turning out to be nearly as destructive as the mindless deregulation of the Reagan years. The legislation dismantled two ineffective regulatory agencies—the Federal Savings and Loan Insurance Corp. and the Federal Home Loan Bank Board—and replaced them with many new ones. Heading the list was the Resolution Trust Corp. Run by an Oversight Board comprising the secretaries of Treasury and Housing and Urban Development and the Federal Reserve chairman, the RTC's mission was to run the S&L cleanup and manage bankrupt S&Ls. Other agencies set up by the legislation included the Federal Housing Finance Board, to oversee home lending by regional Federal Home Loan Banks; the Resolution Funding Corp., to sell $30 billion in bonds to finance part of the S&L cleanup cost; the Bank Insurance Fund, to receive deposit insurance premiums from banks; the Savings Association Insurance Fund, to receive insurance funds from surviving S&Ls; and the Office of Thrift Supervision, set up within the Treasury Department to regulate federally chartered S&Ls.

A reflection of the disarray was Daniel Kearney's decision in February to quit his post as the first president and chief executive of FIRREA'S Oversight Board. A major reason, he said, was confusion over who in the bureaucratic maze was responsible for what. A few days later, Fred Alt, the board's vice president for finance, followed suit. Despite such departures, however, the Bush administration remained complacent. A low point was reached in mid-March when U.S. District Judge Royce C. Lamberth barred the federal takeover of an Illinois S&L on the ground that neither the acting director of the Office of Thrift Supervision, Salvatore R. Martoche, nor the original director, M. Danny Wall,

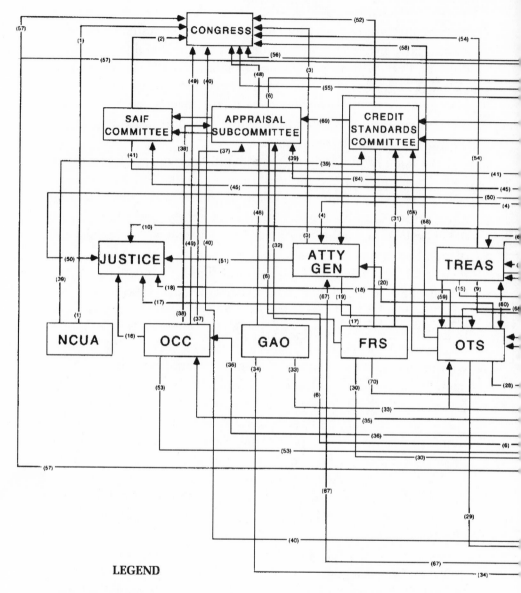

LEGEND

1. Enforce. Report § 918
2. Committee Report § 226
3. Enforce. Report § 918
4. Bridge Bank Activity § 214
5. Annual Reports § 501
6. Approve 2 Board Members § 501
7. Approve 4 Board Members § 702
8. Appoint 6 Comm. Members § 1205
9. Purchase FHLMC Oblig. § 731
10. Crim. Refer. § 918
11. Backup Funds § 511
12. Serve on BOD § 501
13. Preserve Minority Shops § 308
14. Report on Rec./Conserv. Activity § 212 Can
    Borrow 5B with Treasury's OK § 218; Quarterly
    Operating Plans & Forcast § 220
15. Supplement SAIF Fund § 211; FSLIC Fund § 215
16. Crim. Refer. § 918
17. Crim. Refer. § 918
18. Crim. Refer. § 918
19. Bridge Bank Activity § 214

20. Into. on Holding Co. § 301
21. Approve Corp. Debt Activity § 222; Preserve
    Minority Shops § 308
22. Notify of Ins. Trans. § 206; Collect
    Fees/Assessments § 208; § 301 New S&L Appl. §
    212; Enforce. Action § 912 Subsidiary Activity §
    220; Report on Rec./Conserv. Action § 212
23. Help Fund SAIF § 211
24. Serve on BOD § 702
25. Reimburse RTC Property § 501
26. Help Fund § 511
27. Dist. Bank Allocation § 511
28. Serve on BOD § 203
29. Appoint Rec./Conserv. § 212
30. Serve on BOD § 501
31. Comm. Member § 1205
32. Comm. Member § 1101
33. Ann. Audit § 301 Audit of BIF. SAIF. FSLIC
    Funds; Old FSLIC Cases Ann. § 219, 501
34. Ann. Audit § 501, 511, 702, 731
35. Report on Rec./Conserv. Activity § 212

NTERRELATIONSHIPS

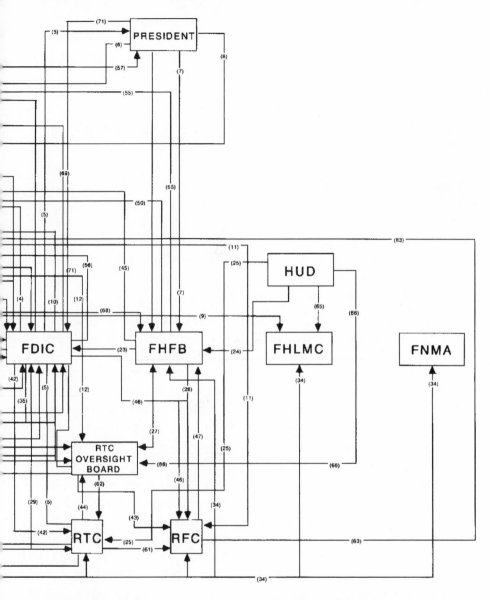

Civil Money Penalty Regs. § 907
Comm. Mem. § 1101
Comm. Mem. § 1205
Comm. Mem. § 1101, 1205
Reports and Appearances § 501
Report to BODs § 226
SAIF Funding Help § 211
Set Dir./Dispose Assets § 511
Reports/Funding Requests § 501
Rep. From Dist. Banks § 226
Send FSLIC Fund Money § 215
Issue Stocks § 511
Report Audit Findings
Enforce. Report § 918
Crim. Refer. § 918
Crim. Refer. § 918
Enforce. Report § 918; Bank Ser./Fee § 1002
Serve on BODs § 203
Ann. Reports on Fed. Financial Asst./Risk Assess.
§ 1403, 1404

55. Ann. Reports on Housing, Enforcement, Activities
    & Advances, Home Mortgage Disclosure Act §
    721, 918, 1211 Title VII
56. Ann. Report on BIF, SAIF, FSLIC Funds § 220;
    Enforce. Report § 918
57. Ann. Report on RFC Activity § 511
58. Ann. Report on Activity § 301; Enforce. Report §
    918
59. Oversee § 301
60. Preserve Minority Shops § 308
61. Issue Cert. § 501; Pay Under Special Cond. § 511
62. Oversee Activity § 501
63. Pay Back Assets on Dissolution § 511
64. Comm. Mem. § 1101; § 1205
65. Regulator § 731
66. Serve on BOD § 501
67. Bridge Bank Activity § 214
68. Request Advances § 714
69. Comm. Mem. § 1101; § 1205
70. Bank Holding Co. Approval § 206
71. Appoint 3 Board Members § 203

who had resigned under pressure earlier in the month, had been nominated by Bush or confirmed by the Senate. The decision, which the administration immediately appealed, unleashed a wave of litigation from other S&Ls fighting federal takeovers. The decision also prompted Bush to nominate a permanent OTS director, a move that he should have taken with Wall's departure. The wrangle only underscored the administration's inept management of the bailout effort and served to delay planned seizures of foundering thrifts still in operation. The eventual cost of this to taxpayers was estimated to be roughly $100 million a day. In May, struggling to sell off $16.4 billion of real estate and other holdings of seized S&Ls at a faster pace, Seidman gained approval to slash the asking prices as much as 30 percent below the appraised value. The move upset the troubled real estate industry but did little to help the federal sales effort.

Whatever the eventual amount of bailout money required, the burden inevitably will fall on taxpayers; as the budget deficit deepens, so will the Treasury's borrowing needs, further burdening the economy. Inevitably as well, depositors seeking high rates of return will have to assume greater risk. Even after the 1989 bailout legislation, S&L insurance still amounted to "a delegation to private enterprises of the government's sovereign right to coin money," according to James Tobin, Yale's Nobel-laureate economist.[6] A better solution would be for the federal government to continue to provide full guarantees on deposits invested in high-grade securities of up to medium-term maturity, say up to five years, but to provide, perhaps in stages, less insurance or possibly none on higher-yielding but riskier deposits. A precedent of sorts can be found in the auto industry, where insurance premiums long have varied according to the risk characteristics of individual drivers. To limit insurance to one deposit per customer also would be a step in the right direction.

Nor would a reduction in deposit-insurance levels necessarily mean a rerun of the financial panics that occurred before such insurance was introduced in the early 1930s. Circumstances are very different now, with gold no longer a form of money in the United States and the Federal Reserve a far more experienced lender of last resort than in the 1930s, readier to supply strapped financial institutions with whatever funds fearful depositors might wish to withdraw. The insurance guarantee was initiated in 1934 at $5,000 per account and then raised repeatedly: in 1950 to $10,000, in 1966 to $15,000, in 1974 to $40,000, and in 1980 to $100,000, where it remained under Bush, whose administration seemed uninclined to take a first step toward bringing the ceiling back down. In fact, the guarantee in practice was even more generous than the $100,000 figure indicated, because the government was already bailing out all depositors, regardless of size, at any institution deemed, in Seidman's words, "too big to fail." The precedent was set in 1984 when regulators opted to cover all deposits at Chicago's failing Continental Bank & Trust, rather than risk a banking panic. By 1990, the government in effect was insuring nearly everybody, which meant more than $3 trillion in deposits at commercial banks, S&Ls still in operation, and credit unions.

Perhaps the best solution left to Bush and Congress, but one which was not being pursued, was to eliminate the savings-and-loan industry altogether by asking for legislation to fold surviving S&L units into stronger commercial banks. S&Ls were created by Congress to alleviate the housing shortage after World War II, but with money flowing into housing from pension funds, insurance companies, commercial banks, and even individual investors, as well as from assorted federal agencies, S&Ls had become a costly anachronism. Thomas M. Garrett, president of the National Bank of Commerce in Memphis, said, "It is an industry that has lost its purpose, its capital and, to a great extent, its integrity," which grew only because of "its unregulated franchise to borrow money with taxpayer-protected guarantees, despite inadequate capital."[7]

Meanwhile, the government's financial health continued to deteriorate. By the start of 1990, the ratio of government receipts to the interest expense on government borrowing was below 6:1, down from 10:1 when Reagan took office and 15:1 in the late 1960s. Moreover, about 33 percent of the government's receivables, such as overdue debt from the Farmers Home Administration, was delinquent. The delinquency rate was 24 percent as recently as 1987 and below 15 percent in 1983. And, of course, the true budget deficit was swelling rapidly, making a mockery of Gramm-Rudman-Hollings. By mid-1990, with the deficit rising, the law's deficit target of $100 billion for the fiscal year ending in September was utterly beyond reach and the fiscal 1991 target of $64 billion was barely higher than the deficit recently run up in a single month. The law called for a further deficit decline to $28 billion in fiscal 1992 and a balanced budget the year after that.

A rising new worry was the health of commercial banking. William Seidman, the chairman of the Federal Deposit Insurance Corporation, told Congress at the end of July that the agency's Bank Insurance Fund would probably lose some $2 billion over the course of the year, draining its reserves to $11 billion, the lowest level in its fifty-seven years and less than 60 cents for every $100 of bank deposits. Two weeks after this testimony, the agency moved to increase the premiums that banks must pay it for their insurance coverage by $1.1 billion, a 30 percent boost.

F O R overburdened state and local governments, meanwhile, Bush was urging steps that could only worsen their predicament. In March, Transportation Secretary Samuel Skinner proposed a plan called "Moving America: New Directions, New Opportunities," which urged cutting the federal share of spending on all federally aided highway projects to about 75 percent from as high as 90 percent, with states paying an increased share. The plan came on the heels of what was becoming typical Bush rhetoric— in this case, a well-publicized warning by the president that the transportation system was "beginning to break down" and "we cannot afford inadequate, inefficient transportation." He called for "essential new capacity" in transportation "to meet critical national needs." Assuredly, the needs were national in scope. However, the president would force on already-strapped states and localities more and more of the burden for such rising expenses as police and fire protection, sanitation, education, and repair of infrastructure. In New York, for example, local communities were deriving only a quarter of their funds through federal and state aid, against about 40 percent in the early 1980s. As a result, most New York communities were having to raise real estate taxes, among other painful measures; since 1987, real estate taxes in the state had risen, on the average, about 25 percent and the New York real estate industry, by no coincidence, had entered a recession.

But the sagging infrastructure called instead for a larger federal role. Near the end of Reagan's presidency, the overall expense for building and maintaining roads was running at about $66 billion a year, less than two thirds of which was covered by road-user taxes and tolls; the rest was the burden of state and local governments. A comprehensive federal system of increased, precisely targeted user fees was needed; the Brookings Institution, for instance, proposed in mid-1989 a pavement-wear tax for heavy trucks, to be based on axle weight, to "cover the damage that a truck causes to a road."[8] But there was no follow-up on such proposals from the Bush administration or Congress, even though the decline of the infrastructure was a national problem affecting productivity and ultimately living standards across the country.

To make matters worse, billions of dollars in federal trust funds were on tap, but not used, for work on the infrastructure. The highway and airport trust funds, for instance, showed surpluses totaling over $4 billion in 1989, but this money was not spent for highways or airports but was held back so as to keep down the deficit.[9] The federal share of spending for mass transit—a sensible answer to clogged highways and pollution from car exhaust—had fallen by about 50 percent in the Reagan years. As a result, transit systems in many regions had deteriorated badly, but the Bush administration made no moves to reverse the trend, and the share of such spending accounted for by states and localities rose to more than 80 percent from about 60 percent a decade earlier. In the process, more and more states came under increased financial strain. In March, for instance, Standard & Poor's Corp. lowered its credit rating for New York's long-term bonds to A from AA−, a two-notch drop. By making it costlier for the state to borrow, the rating cut placed a further financial strain on the state, whose deficit, for perspective, roughly matched the cost of building two Stealth bombers, a plane which was of doubtful utility even before the Cold War ended, but which the Bush administration continued to promote.

Meanwhile, the operating deficits of most states and localities were rising sharply. On a combined basis, the deficits reached a record annual rate of $52 billion in early 1990. In the mid-1980s, in contrast, there was a combined surplus of more than $20 billion. A typical result of this financial deterioration, and the lack of federal help, was that many states were compelled to slash food allotments for poor families. Texas, for instance, lowered its cereal allotment for children under three years old to twenty-four ounces a month from thirty-six and dropped 27,000 recipients from the rolls. California reduced its monthly allotment of fruit juice for three-to-five-year-olds by one-half. Iowa removed four thousand recipients from its food program and Missouri cut fourteen thousand from its program.

The Bush administration was also unresponsive to the deterioration taking place within federal agencies. In Reagan's last year, the Internal Revenue Service was some $400 million short of what it claimed was needed for it to function properly. But little was done, so that under Bush the agency was unable to audit dozens of returns from large corporations that would otherwise have come under close scrutiny. Similarly, IRS offices in the mid-Atlantic area were compelled for several months to subsist with so little computer-printer paper that when a group of tax-shelter operators in the area offered to settle a big case for $100 million, the office simply could not process the required paperwork. In early 1990, IRS Commissioner Fred T. Goldberg told a congressional hearing that about 40 percent of the answers that the agency provided by telephone to inquiring taxpayers who managed to get through to its overloaded staff of "tax assisters" were incorrect. Only 55 percent of the callers, he added, were able to get through on the first call.

Meanwhile, the Federal Bureau of Investigation early in Bush's presidency asked for enough money to take on 425 additional agents to investigate the many scams conducted at failed S&Ls. But the agency received only enough for 201 more agents. In Dallas, an area hit particularly hard by S&L failures, federal investigators were forced to sift through some seven million documents related to improper S&L activities, and to help they sought sixty-four additional FBI agents but received, after much pleading, only thirty-seven. San Diego, facing similar problems on a smaller scale, asked for five agents and got none. Fraud and other criminal activity were found to be involved in "more than 60 percent of all the S&Ls we've had to take over," FDIC Chairman William Seidman reported in March 1990. And much of the money had disappeared. In Houston, Henry Oncken, a U.S. attorney, reported that in his southern Texas district federal courts in criminal prosecutions had ordered $2.6 million in restitution during 1989, but by April 1990 only $29,000 had been collected. "A lot of the money is in Switzerland and other places, and you'll never see it," predicted H. Joe Selby, a former director of thrift supervision for the Southwest.

To reinvigorate federal agencies, Bush would have had to reallocate funds away from defense—and in doing so take on a large Republican contingent dead set on continuing to dismantle the federal bureaucracy. But he avoided such a confrontation, and so most agencies remained underfunded. Such a tight leash might be expected at least to reduce bureaucratic waste, but wastefulness persisted. In early 1990, a Justice Department audit of the Drug Enforcement Agency, for example, found widespread violations of federal procurement rules, including overpaying suppliers and awarding too many no-bid contracts. One DEA supplier received $22,500 for three video cameras, for use in aircraft surveillance, which according to the audit should have cost only $7,230. The audit also found that ten of twenty-five no-bid contracts awarded should have been competitive.

A business-as-usual approach was evident in the administration's budget planning. The 1,569-page document that Bush submitted to Congress on January 29, 1990, contained much rhetoric about fiscal problems. An eloquent introductory essay by Budget Director Richard G. Darman warned, for instance, that as much as $50 billion a year might be needed for "hidden Pac-Men," by which he meant sudden, unforeseen increases in such costs as federal bailouts of troubled thrifts. Apart from the S&L bailout costs, the government insured $2.7 trillion in checking and savings accounts, $1.3 trillion in pensions, crop programs, and foreign investments, and $1.6 trillion in assorted types of loans for housing, students, small businesses, and agriculture.

The body of the budget document, however, was replete with overly optimistic fiscal assumptions. It also assumed appreciably faster economic growth and lower interest rates than most private analysts were forecasting, and it envisioned multibillion-

dollar savings through greatly improved efficiency within the bureaucracy—for example, a $2.5 billion saving through "manage-
ment reforms" at the IRS, $1.5 billion through a speedier
procedure for Medicare payments, and $2.3 billion through un-
specified "management savings" in defense.

The gap between the Bush administration's rhetoric and performance was apparent during a March hearing of the Senate
Finance Committee, when Treasury Secretary Nicholas F. Brady
declined to support a proposal by two senators from his own
Republican party for an excise tax on capital gains of pension
funds on sales of assets held for less than six months. The proposal was aimed at curbing stock market speculation and foster-
ing a longer-term approach to investing, goals that Brady had long
endorsed in speeches. Faced with the prospect of actual legislation, however, the secretary reversed field, professing that new
"taxation should be viewed as a last resort." Instead, he talked
vaguely of the government's responsibility to "make clear that the
fiduciary duty to maximize return for fund beneficiaries is best
achieved by long-term investing, not short-term trading."

Meanwhile, new problems were beginning to arise which required, but were not receiving, attention. By the spring of 1990,
long before the Iraqi takeover of Kuwait, oil production in the
United States was falling at an alarming rate while imports of
petroleum products were rising sharply. In January alone, oil
imports surged to nearly $6 billion, a 44 percent increase reflect-
ing a record inflow of 291 million barrels. Foreign oil accounted
for 54 percent of U.S. consumption, also a record, and domestic
production dropped to its lowest level in twenty-five years. Yet
the Bush administration showed little concern over this dependency on foreign suppliers and continued to oppose measures,
such as a tax on petroleum imports, to encourage self-sufficiency
and reduce the budget deficit. Hastening the production decline
were 1986 tax changes that eliminated some tax shelters long
enjoyed by oil producers. There also was growing wastefulness
among drillers. The Department of Energy found that some eighteen thousand wells were abandoned annually after only about
one-third of their potential had been recovered. Americans were
consuming over 25 barrels of oil per capita each year, compared

to 14 barrels per each Japanese, 13 per each West German, 12 per each Italian, and 11 per each Briton.

Insurance was another industry that needed closer scrutiny. In February, a House Energy and Commerce subcommittee launched hearings on whether the federal government should play a role in regulating insurance companies, which had long been under state control. Prompting the hearings was an alarming rise in insurance insolvencies. Between 1969 and 1987, these amounted to $2.2 billion, but the total soared by another $5 billion in 1988 and 1989. This rise coincided with an increase in insurers' holdings of junk bonds, many of which were turning out to be worthless, or nearly so. Yet such risky holdings were generally permitted as investments for insurers, since in most states there was still an "appalling lack of regulatory controls," as the committee chairman, John Dingell of Michigan, said. The subcommittee concluded, on the basis of an eighteen-month investigation, that "the parallels between the present situation in the insurance industry and the early stages of the savings and loan debacle are both obvious and deeply disturbing."[10]

Insurance companies, unlike S&Ls, are not federally insured. One large insurer, the New York unit of First Executive Corp., with nearly half its assets in junk bonds at the start of 1990, suffered a surge of redemptions from nervous policyholders. Showing concern, the National Association of Insurance Commissioners in April urged individual state regulators to set limits within their borders on how much of an insurer's assets could be in junk bonds. At the time, New York was one of only several states with such a limit, set at 20 percent. In 1989, insurance companies accounted for roughly a third of junk-bond purchases, and at the start of 1990 they owned close to $40 billion of the risky securities.

Excessive regulation can deaden business activity, of course, as communism has proved. But under Reagan the government had cut back too much, encouraging abuse by private businesses. His administration's push to deregulate in the pharmaceutical industry, for instance, had led to generic-drug scandals, including falsified company reports to the Food and Drug Administration, whose staff in the 1980s dwindled to less than 7,500 from 8,000-

plus under Carter. Moreover, this shrinkage occurred despite the spread of AIDS, which demanded more and more FDA attention, and despite two dozen new laws that in theory increased the agency's regulatory duties. By the time Bush was in the White House, even such major drug companies as Merck, Upjohn, Johnson & Johnson, and Pfizer were urging that the FDA's ranks be restrengthened.

A still more egregious example of mindless deregulation in the 1980s involved cable television. In 1984, cable operators—who already enjoyed regional monopolies—were allowed to raise prices virtually at will. By 1990, as a result, cable rates were roughly twice as high as they would have been if the operators had faced competition within their areas. With price deregulation, franchises valued at $600 per subscriber soon were commanding $2,500. Millionaire cable operators swiftly became multimillionaires, with cable customers footing the bill.

As for the deregulated airline industry, even normally conservative Republican politicians were urging by 1989 that the carriers be placed under stricter supervision. Higher fares and reduced choice for flyers were among the effects of deregulation. When Reagan came to Washington, there were nineteen major airlines in operation in the United States; when he left there were only eight. By no coincidence, an Economic Policy Institute study found in early 1990 that travel costs for the average airline passenger, adjusted for the cost of jet fuel, which—no thanks to deregulation—fell in the 1980s, had risen nearly 3 cents per mile since the industry's deregulation. Moreover, since deregulation ushered in a more circuitous hub-and-spoke routing system for planes, the cost per trip was 8 percent to 33 percent higher, depending on the route. Still, Bush seemed unconcerned.

Reagan, on his third day as president, appointed Bush, then his vice president, to head a so-called Task Force on Regulatory Relief, whose aim was to spot areas in apparent need of less governmental control, or none at all. The move to deregulate may have begun with the Carter White House, but it was Reagan and Bush who gave it impetus. Industries where federal control was subsequently eased included not only airlines and drugs but telephones and trucking. In all, between 1982 and 1988, full-time civilian employment in the federal government, not including the

Pentagon, edged down to 1,004,481, a 5 percent drop. Jobs disappeared at the departments of Agriculture, Commerce, Education, Energy, Health and Human Services, Housing and Urban Development, Interior, Labor, and Transportation. There were also declines at the Tennessee Valley Authority, the General Services Administration, and the Office of Personnel Management. Bush later recalled his work with the task force as among his "proudest accomplishments as vice president."

Whatever Bush's accomplishments as vice president, the fact remains that in the early part of his own presidency most of the problems that festered under Reagan grew worse—from the pileup of debt to the deterioration of health care to the decay of the infrastructure. Moreover, new problems arose, such as deepening financial difficulties in insurance, banking, and state and local governments. In short, a new man was in the White House but all the old difficulties persisted and worrisome new ones were emerging.

CHAPTER FIVE

LAGGING LEADERS

There is a time in every presidency where you gotta start doing things that are unpopular with some groups. Outside forces come into play and the joyride is over. Bush's time had to come. It's a wonder it lasted so long.

—A Republican strategist quoted in *The Washington Post*, June 28, 1990.

O N C E Bush was in the White House himself, his deregulatory zeal appeared to diminish somewhat, but this mainly reflected a response to political pressures. Even such Bush allies as New York's Republican Senator Alphonse D'Amato declared at the end of Reagan's presidency that "I don't see deregulation as a driving force anymore." Earlier, Nicholas F. Brady, the former stockbroker and New Jersey senator who was to become Bush's treasury secretary, had urged stiffer regulation of the stock market in the wake of the October 1987 crash. Two years later, as treasury secretary, Brady again urged at a Senate hearing that the stock market come under stricter federal regulation. He proposed that the chairman of the Securities and Exchange Commission be given the power to halt trading of shares in the event of a crisis, financial or otherwise, and that brokerage firms be required to report to the SEC the identity of all major buyers and sellers of stocks and stock options, as well as the financial condition of all of their affiliates.

But much of this was grandstanding, and little more was done. The SEC had already begun to prod securities dealers to police their own ranks more closely. Reflecting this, four major exchanges—the New York and American stock exchanges, the National Association of Securities Dealers, overseer of the over-the-counter market, and the Chicago Board Options Exchange—brought a combined total of five hundred disciplinary actions resulting in public sanctions in 1988, nearly double the number a year earlier. And at the Federal Reserve Board, examiners had quietly started to "classify" bank loans made for any leveraged buyout in which sales of company assets appeared necessary to service future interest costs. This meant, in effect, that the money loaned out could not be considered part of a bank's capital, which made further lending costlier. The Fed's move was a key reason for the withdrawal of bank lending in a proposed buyout of UAL Corp.; this withdrawal, in turn, was widely cited as the trigger for a 190-point drop in the Dow Jones Industrial Average on October 13, 1989.

Right after that big decline, John J. Phelan, then chairman of the New York Stock Exchange, grudgingly lent his support to the proposal making its way through Congress giving the SEC authority in severe market declines to suspend program trading. This practice, blamed for causing severe market volatility, uses computers to capitalize on temporary differences in stock-price indexes traded in separate markets. In early November, the NYSE voluntarily adopted a series of trading limits designed to curb program trading. For example, a steep drop in the Dow Jones Industrial Average would trigger a halt in program trading. Around the same time, officials of the Chicago Mercantile Exchange, a major marketplace for futures trading of stock indexes, announced a similar series of halts. So in the world of securities trading, the freewheeling practices of the Reagan years were yielding ever so slowly to increased regulation. For example, on August 6, 1990, on the heels of Iraq's move into Kuwait, the Dow Jones Industrial Average fell 93.91 points, setting off various new circuit breakers which helped slow the slide. For instance, the New York Stock Exchange restricted index arbitrage, a form of program trading, after the Dow Jones average had fallen 50 points.

Elsewhere, regulatory moves were well publicized, but again were slow to be implemented and generally of little consequence.

In the auto industry, Bush's new transportation secretary, Samuel Skinner, proposed tougher safety requirements, including stronger roofs and lap-and-shoulder belts for minivans and light trucks. Skinner also ordered that 1990-model car fleets be required to average a minimum of 27.5 miles per gallon, up from the long-time standard of twenty-six miles. In the appliance business, the Energy Department ordered that refrigerators and freezers built after 1992 would have to consume 25 percent less energy than 1989 models, which would also save consumers some $20 yearly, on the average, in electricity costs. The new Labor secretary, Elizabeth Dole, urged rules under which the government could close various types of mines for repeated safety violations. And in November, her Occupational Health and Safety Administration proposed its highest-ever corporate fine, a $7.3 million levy against two USX Corp. plants charged with health-and-safety violations. In the same month, the Federal Railroad Administration, responsible for rail safety procedures, increased its staff to thirty-two from twenty-eight—hardly a major change. But the number was scheduled to rise further to two hundred under legislation introduced in Congress by Thomas A. Luken, the Ohio Democrat chairing a House Energy and Commerce subcommittee on transportation and hazardous waste.

The Bush administration professed concern for firmer antitrust policy, which was virtually nonexistent under Reagan. In November 1989, James F. Rill, the new assistant attorney general in charge of the Justice Department's antitrust division, declared, "I don't want to draw comparisons with the prior [Reagan] administration, but I do take a pragmatic approach to antitrust enforcement." He would require, he warned, "hard evidence before I make a decision not to challenge a merger that otherwise looks like it could have anticompetitive effects." Under Rill, the Justice Department opposed and eventually managed to block a plan by American Airlines and Delta Air Lines to set up a joint reservation system, as well as an Eastern Air Lines proposal to sell its gates at Philadelphia to USAir, which in the opinion of the government would have lessened airline competition in that city. But by and large, Rill's declaration was simply more administration grandstanding. Judged by its actions, the Bush White House showed little more concern about antitrust than Reagan's White House.

This attitude persisted despite growing public pressure for a tougher antitrust stance. The National Association of Attorneys General had begun seeking a stricter policy late in Reagan's presidency, when the organization of state officials drafted guidelines to challenge large corporate takeovers already approved by Reagan's Justice Department or the Federal Trade Commission. One such challenge in California led to the eventual blocking of a merger of supermarket chains that would have left the companies in control of some 50 percent of the grocery business in the southern part of the state and would probably have cost consumers as much as $400 million in higher prices.

Though its own budget was tight, the Internal Revenue Service was getting stricter about tax exemptions. In November, the agency stripped more than one hundred organizations of their exemptions, including a tennis group, a skier education foundation, and a "music" ministry. But in larger matters, the agency was not even managing to tread water. In 1989, it had funds enough to audit only 25.52 percent of large corporations and a mere 1.61 percent of small ones. A decade earlier, by comparison, it audited 47.82 percent of large firms and 7.42 percent of small ones. This declining ability to conduct audits was a major reason that the agency missed over $100 billion annually in potential tax revenues. "It will take many years to restore audit coverage to appropriate levels, and it's time we start," IRS Commissioner Goldberg told Congress in April 1990, but with the budget deficit setting records, there was little to be done about his plea.

There was also much talk—but little action—about a tougher stance in disputes over international investment and trade. But again, there was much grandstanding, with the focus on Japan, which along with the war on drugs was always fair game for U.S. politicians, especially now that the Russians were no longer a plausible enemy. In October 1989, Bush's number-two man at the Treasury, Deputy Secretary John Robson, warned in Tokyo that while the United States still welcomed Japanese investors, the welcome mat would be withdrawn unless Japan did more to welcome foreign investors. He spoke of the U.S. need for a sterner negotiating position with Japan and claimed that "we may be losing control over our economic independence."

Robson's talk came a few days after Sony Corp.'s $3.4 billion takeover of Columbia Pictures Entertainment Inc. and Mitsubishi Estate New York Inc.'s announcement that it would pay nearly $1 billion for control of the Rockefeller Group Inc., which owned Rockefeller Center and other famous buildings in Manhattan. In the wake of Robson's warning, Japanese buyers shied away from bidding on the 110-story Sears Tower in Chicago. They feared their purchase of the world's tallest building might stir up too much anti-Japanese sentiment among Americans, which surveys showed was rising. Sixty-nine percent of those queried in one poll said they regarded the trade imbalance between the United States and Japan as "a serious issue" that required corrective action. About two thirds urged outright quotas for Japanese products aimed at the American market, 61 percent called as well for higher tariffs, and 59 percent urged restricting the flow of U.S. technology to Japan. A remarkable 68 percent viewed the economic challenge by Japan as the most serious threat to America's future, while only 22 percent cited the military threat from the Soviet Union; the survey was taken in August, before the opening of the Berlin Wall and the Bush-Gorbachev summit at Malta.[1]

Responding to such sentiments, Bush appointees kept sounding a hard negotiating line. In Washington, U.S. Trade Representative Carla A. Hills and her deputy, S. Linn Williams, were talking tough, and in Tokyo, Ambassador Michael H. Armacost, a professor turned diplomat who also voiced a sterner line on trade, replaced the aging former senator Mike Mansfield as the American ambassador. As early as May, the new Bush team, acting under the so-called Super 301 provisions of the Omnibus Trade and Competitiveness Act of 1988, labeled Japan a "priority" example of an unfair trader in such areas as forest products and supercomputers. A short while later, talks were launched between the two nations to begin removing trade impediments. The U.S. list of complaints was extended, for example, to Japan's system of product distribution, which tended to restrict sales of U.S. goods in Japan and U.S. ownership of Japanese firms. Another target: Japanese tax rules on land use, which served to protect the nation's inefficient farming sector against agricultural imports from the United States and elsewhere.

Some minor headway was evident by late 1989, when Japan's Ministry of International Trade and Industry agreed to alter the distribution system along less protectionist lines and to submit changes for approval by the Diet, Japan's parliament. Around the same time, ninety-nine Japanese construction firms agreed to pay the United States $32.6 million to settle U.S. charges that they had rigged bids on several projects undertaken at a U.S. naval base in Japan. On Christmas Eve, Japanese officials opted to allow tax credits to companies in Japan that increased their imports from the United States and other countries of such big-ticket manufactured goods as machinery, motor vehicles, and computers. A short while later, *Nihon Keizai Shimbun,* Japan's leading business newspaper, found in a survey of ten thousand Japanese that over 80 percent agreed with U.S. criticism that Japan's economy should be made more open to foreign goods. The prevailing view was that this would improve Japan's international relationships as well as living conditions for Japanese consumers.

The harder U.S. line was sounded again in October, with Carla Hills challenging a plan by the European Community mandating that at least half of the bloc's television programming be produced in Europe. She labeled the EC proposal "deplorable" and "blatantly protectionist" and warned of retaliation by the United States if it was implemented. And in November, Congress began considering a bill that would limit investment in the United States by any nation with barriers to American investors. At the time, would-be U.S. investors in Japan were bitter that Japan had thrown obstacles in their way. T. Boone Pickens complained loudly that Japan was blocking his efforts to obtain seats on the board of a Japanese automotive parts producer of which he was the largest shareholder.

But the reality was that little changed. Japan's direct investments in the United States in 1989 rose roughly 40 percent to $75 billion, twice the level of only two years earlier. The percentage of cars sold in the United States that were Japanese was nearing 30 percent, and Japan continued to sport a huge trade surplus of some $50 billion with the United States. Even so, in April 1990

Bush quietly removed Japan from its unfair-trader status. Meanwhile, the ranks of U.S. trade negotiators were riddled with people with past or present ties to Japanese corporations, hardly
conducive to a firm U.S. trade position and a practice that would
not be tolerated in the Japanese government. Two top deputies in
the U.S. trade representative's office once worked for Japanese
firms, and Carla Hills herself once advised Matsushita Electric
Co. Her daughter remained on a legal team helping a Japanese typewriter maker under investigation by the Commerce Department for dumping, while her husband remained a business
partner of the head of Nissan Motor Co.'s lobbying firm in Washington. Altogether, about twenty former high-ranking U.S. trade
officials went on to work for foreign clients, largely Japanese,
between the early 1970s and 1990. Republican Senator John Heinz
of Pennsylvania labeled the pattern "a national tragedy," and
early in 1990 Senator Lloyd Bentsen, the Texas Democrat, called
for hearings on such "revolving-door" conflicts. But this was
mainly political smoke; the White House was unconcerned and
the practice persisted.[2]

A S   difficulties multiplied for Bush, public attitudes began to
shift. Many Americans seemed to be drawing ahead of their political leaders in understanding the severity and urgency of the
nation's economic and social problems. If self-indulgence marked
the 1980s, increased concern about the future seemed the watch-
word of the new decade. A Gallup Poll found that 83 percent of
the population was distressed by how many people were living
below the poverty line, and only 33 percent approved of Washington's handling of the problem. Another poll found that 80 percent
of the population felt protecting the environment had grown more
important than the economic costs this might entail. By comparison, only 51 percent held this view in a similar survey taken at
the start of Reagan's presidency.[3]

Worry about job security was also on the rise. Since 1983, some
4.7 million workers who had held their jobs for at least three
years had been fired; about a third of these took pay cuts of at
least 20 percent in their next jobs, and about 25 percent remained
out of work. With labor unions weak and foreign competition

strong, companies were reducing long-standing fringe benefits. The percentage of major corporations paying the full cost of hospital room and board for their employees fell to 29 percent from 53 percent in Reagan's final term. Corporations depended ever more heavily on temporary workers, who received fewer benefits and less pay than regular employees. Of nearly seventeen million jobs created between 1983 and mid-1989, some three million were temporary. By no coincidence, company loyalty eroded. Some 63 percent of workers felt less loyal to their employers than a decade earlier, 50 percent expected to be at another job within five years, and 57 percent believed that their employers had grown less loyal to them.[4]

What made matters worse was the widening disparity between the pay of top executives and pay of other employees. During the Reagan years, the average compensation of chief executive officers of the *Fortune* 500 industrial companies rose about 150 percent, more than triple the average increase for production workers at the same companies. The pattern was continuing with Bush in the White House. In 1989, the median pay of the chief executives of the nation's one hundred largest industrial corporations rose about 10 percent. That was twice the median profit gain of the hundred firms and about three times comparable pay rise of the other employees. Compensation in 1989 for the ten highest-paid CEOs in America ranged from $53.9 million for Craig O. McCaw of McCaw Cellular Communications to $8.9 million for August A. Busch III of Anheuser-Busch, the beer producer.

Chief executives of large U.S. corporations, on the average, were earning over 50 percent more than their Japanese counterparts, 90 percent more than their counterparts in Britain and West Germany, and four times more than top South Korean executives. At Merrill Lynch & Co., the large New York–based securities firm, the chief executive, William A. Schreyer, often used a company helicopter to and from his Princeton, New Jersey, home while the firm in early 1990 was laying off some 3,500 employees and charging $470 million against earnings, mainly on account of real-estate leases gone sour. Around the same time, top executives of Drexel Burnham—soon to go bankrupt—were paying themselves some $350 million in bonuses, some of which exceeded $10 million per individual. Outside directors, supposedly monitoring chief executives' pay, readily endorsed exorbitant executive pay packages as their own pay and perks for attending board meetings spiraled upward.

The pay squeeze for workers, meanwhile, was especially intense in manufacturing. In 1982, a recession year, 45 percent of all manufacturing workers who negotiated contracts settled for terms that reduced their wages at least 6 percent in the first year of the agreement, after taking inflation into account. In 1986, amid the longest business expansion in the country's peacetime history, 70 percent of manufacturing workers settled for terms that reduced their first-year wages, further evidence that rank-and-file Americans were lowering their living standards in order to keep their jobs. The hourly pay of American production workers was no longer higher than that of many of their overseas counterparts; in many instances, it was lower. In contrast, as recently as 1985, the U.S. average of $12.96 an hour compared with Japan's $6.47, West Germany's $9.56, Italy's $7.40, France's $7.52, and Britain's $6.19.

As painful as the pay squeeze was, it served along with more automated production facilities to help competitiveness, making U.S. labor cheaper. By the time Bush was president, U.S. steel producers, for example, were operating at an average cost per ton of about a third less than in 1982. USX, the nation's largest steel maker, had managed to slash its work force by 75 percent and its labor costs to 20 cents per dollar of sales from 42 cents. While many USX operations had been closed in the 1980s as uncompetitive and obsolete, such plants as its Irvin, Pennsylvania, facility were now operating with eighteen shifts a week, up from only eight in the early 1980s. As a result, the average cost of steel sold in the United States when Bush took office was lower for American producers, at $484 a ton, than for such other steel-producing nations as Britain ($491), South Korea ($498), Taiwan ($502), France ($527), West Germany ($545), and Japan ($632).

Meanwhile, the debt burden continued to mount, though the rate of increase had begun to slow. In mid-1989, all debt outstanding in the U.S. economy—owed by consumers, businesses, and government—totaled just over $9.4 trillion, a record sum. But the total was now growing by only 8.3 percent a year, the lowest rate since the early 1970s. Throughout much of the 1980s, debt had been rising by 12 percent to 15 percent. The slowing, moreover, was across-the-board. Federal debt—off the budget as well as on—rose 7.1 percent, state and local government debt 4.9 percent, consumer debt 8.5 percent, and debt in private businesses 11 percent—all lower rates than in the 1980s. Increasing bankruptcies meant caution for the junk-bond market, where the amount of new bonds issued each month fell in the fall of 1989 below $33 billion, down from monthly totals of more than $40 billion in much of the previous three years. Under Reagan, government debt in some months surged more than 20 percent on an annual basis and consumer and business debt rose more than 15 percent.

Farm debt had actually begun to edge down. On a per-farm basis, the amount owed was a still-lofty $63,000. However, at $138.4 billion, the total had dropped 3 percent in the past year and was more than 25 percent below the record readings recorded in the mid-1980s. One reason was simply reduced borrowing by farmers, who have become more cautious about their balance sheets. Other factors were improved farm earnings and substantial write-downs and write-offs of old debt by lenders who were applying more rigorous standards for their loans. Moreover, the value of farmland, reflecting the earnings improvement, was beginning to rise after a prolonged slump. In October, farmland in Illinois, Indiana, and Iowa brought, on the average, 9 percent more than a year earlier, and increases nearly as large were reported in such other key agricultural states as Michigan and Wisconsin.

Some overburdened corporations, in the meantime, were trying to strengthen their debt-laden balance sheets. In August 1989, Turner Broadcasting refinanced $1.4 billion of long-term debt long before the maturity dates of the securities involved, increasing their average maturity to eleven years from only seven and cutting their average interest rate to 11 percent from 14 percent. Around the same time, Holiday Corp. moved to wipe out much of its debt load by trading its Holiday Inns unit to the British firm of Bass in exchange for Bass's assuming some $2.1 billion of Holiday debt, as well as for some of Bass's stock. Also in August, Safeway, the large supermarket chain that had gone private in a Kohlberg Kravis Roberts leveraged buyout in 1986, reported that its debt level was down to $3.1 billion from $5.7 billion three years earlier. The company, moreover, was contemplating a new offering of common stock to strengthen its financial position. Smaller companies were turning more cautious as well. In November, the National Federation of Independent Business, representing some 570,000 small businesses, found that only 7 percent of its members expected difficulty in borrowing in the coming months and the average small firm's debt load was diminishing.

The yearly growth of overall savings—by consumers, businesses, and government—was also beginning at long last to pull ahead of the growth of debt. The margin was slim, with savings growth only $1.6 billion higher than debt growth, but this crossover in mid-1989 marked the first time since early in the decade that savings grew more. The pattern, were it to persist, would leave the United States less dependent on foreign capital to finance borrowing. Reasons for the change were diverse. Business planners were starting to sense, after more than seven years of economic growth, that a recession was more likely. Many executives were beginning to worry that in the long run leveraged buyouts would harm the economy and should be discouraged, even if that meant tougher tax rules.

A survey taken after Bush had been in office only a month found that 84 percent of Americans believed that corporate takeover deals were taking place in a "corrupt environment." Two thirds of those surveyed felt, moreover, that "the federal government must place more and heavier restrictions on leveraged buyouts." Only 23 percent saw any benefit in such activity, while more than a fifth reported that they or an immediate family member worked or had worked for a company involved in a takeover in the past three years. Most claimed the buyout trend was bad, often involving loss of job or of pay, or more stress at work.[5] Still, the administration made no effort to halt the deals.

I N   the labor force, more and more paychecks—except for those of many chief executives—were being tied to performance, and this placed a further squeeze on many workers. While paycheck buying power had been eroding, incentives linked to performance were on the increase. Some 40 percent of union workers, for example, were receiving paychecks tied to their companies' performance, such as profit-related bonuses or reductions. In 1983, only 10 percent of union workers had such arrangements. Labor's increased concern about performance was evident in Anaheim, California, where soon after Bush's inauguration the United Auto Workers endorsed an "employee involvement" campaign. Under it, the union agreed to encourage greater worker-management cooperation on the factory floor. The aim, according to UAW president Owen F. Beiber, was to match "the quality and productivity" of Japanese automakers. Practices once anathema to the UAW were now endorsed, such as the use of small teams of multiskilled workers who would swap jobs with one another and required little or no supervision.

In Bush's first year, greater attention to quality appeared at last to be gaining some results. In November, 52 percent of Americans felt the quality of products made in the United States was clearly superior to five years earlier, while only 15 percent found it worse. Still more encouraging was the finding that 94 percent of Americans rated U.S. products as good or very good. This was higher than the comparable ratings for products from Japan (85 percent), West Germany (64 percent), Canada (49 percent), Taiwan (35 percent), and Mexico (19 percent).[6] Responding to increased corporate concern over quality, forty colleges were offering degrees in quality technology in 1989, up from only nine in 1986. But there was still much to be done. For example, buyers of autos imported from Japan still reported fewer problems per car than buyers of U.S. automobiles. However, the difference had narrowed sharply since the early 1980s.

In the same month, the sagging prestige of the U.S. electronics industry was given a needed lift by a ruling of the Japanese government's patent office that all Japanese chip producers would have to begin paying royalties to Texas Instruments Inc. The patent, valid for a dozen years, seemed likely to generate close to $250 million a year in royalties for the Dallas-based firm, whose scientists in 1958 invented the chip, or tiny integrated circuit, now used in such sophisticated electronic devices as computers and cellular phones. Among the Japanese chip makers that Texas Instruments had sued for payments were such leading names as Toshiba, NEC, Mitsubishi Electric, Hitachi, Fujitsu, Matsushita, and Yamaha. On the automobile front, several U.S.-

based subsidiaries of Japanese manufacturers—Mitsubishi Motors, Honda, Mazda, Toyota, and Nissan—were beginning to export cars from the United States to Japan. Mitsubishi announced plans to ship six thousand of its Eclipse sports cars to Japan from its Normal, Illinois, plant. Honda and Toyota each reported plans to ship some fifty thousand U.S.-built cars to Japan in the early 1990s. Mazda, 25 percent owned by Ford Motor Co., had already shipped seven thousand Probe autos to Japan in 1989, and was planning soon to start shipping some sixty thousand cars a year to Japan from its Flat Rock, Michigan, factory. In June 1990, the Japanese government chose American technology developed by Motorola, Inc., as the standard for its cellular telephone system.

The trade deficit, though still enormous, edged lower in Bush's early months. The deficit for merchandise trade, near $160 billion in 1987, was below $120 billion in 1989 and still declining in 1990. Exports of aircraft, office equipment, and such commodities as aluminum, chemicals, paper, and glass were at last rising briskly, and imports, other than oil, were growing more slowly. In the last quarter of 1989, the volume of steel imported was less than the amount allowed under the industry's import quota system. At the same time, the big surpluses of such powerhouse traders as Japan and South Korea were starting to diminish, and trade deficits were deepening in Britain and Australia.

No small factor in all of this was improved U.S. competitiveness resulting from the dollar's decline and reduced pay rates. American exports were on the rise, and imports, now costlier, were edging down. And the dollar's purchasing power abroad seemed undervalued, suggesting that in fundamental terms the currency was stronger than global foreign-exchange markets so far recognized. The point was underscored in November 1989 in a joint survey by the Commerce Department and Japan's Ministry of International Trade and Industry. Applying prevailing currency exchange rates, the report found that of 122 products, eighty-four cost more in Japan than in the United States. Scotch produced in Britain sold for $20.49 in New York and $41.02 in Tokyo. A cordless telephone made in Japan cost $139.95 in New York and $177.77 in Tokyo. A set of American-made golf clubs cost $420 in New York and $659.15 in Tokyo. A pizza, made locally, brought $8 in New York and $14.08 in Tokyo. A ticket to the movies cost $7.25 in New York and $11.27 in Tokyo. Among the few exceptions to this pattern was a European-made car tire, which sold for $87 in New York and $72.18 in Tokyo.

M E A N W H I L E, changes in the tax rules enacted in 1986, for all the shortcomings of the new law, were at least beginning to extract more revenue from corporations that had managed to freeload during much of the Reagan presidency. In 1982, as many as seventy-two of the nation's 250 largest profitable corporations, using loopholes, paid no federal income tax, but by 1989 only seven of these companies paid no tax. The average corporate tax bill rose in the period to 26.5 percent of profits from 14.3 percent, as the closing of loopholes more than offset a drop in the corporate tax rate to 34 percent from 46 percent. The 1986 legislation also served, however feebly, to channel investment flows more toward productive facilities that enhanced America's competitiveness and away from real estate, where so much money had been placed in the past for reasons that often had more to do with tax avoidance than good investment policy. In the second quarter of 1989, investment in machine tools and other such basics of the production process rose 15 percent annually, after allowing for inflation, while investment in residential construction fell 12 percent. Under the 1986 law, investors could no longer plow, say, $100,000 into a real estate limited partnership and then claim $200,000 in tax deductions. The home-mortgage-interest deduction, still a sacred cow, survived the 1986 act, but not entirely unscathed. Interest on home-mortgage debt above $1 million was ruled no longer deductible.

Even so, when Bush took office the interest deduction on home mortgages was still costing the Treasury about $35 billion a year in forgone tax receipts. And there was more. Property-tax deductions from federal tax bills exceeded $8 billion a year. The deferral of capital gains on the sale of a principal residence cost the federal government nearly $11 billion. The exclusion of capital gains on the sale of a principal residence by anyone fifty-five years old or older cost nearly $4 billion.

The temporary implementation on October 16, 1989, of the so-called sequestration provisions of the Gramm-Rudman-Hollings

Act helped ever so briefly to hold down spending. Cuts in federal outlays of $16.1 billion went into effect after Bush signed an order that afternoon to comply with the deficit-reduction law. The cuts became mandatory after Congress and the administration failed to agree by that date on how to bring the federal deficit for fiscal 1990 below a legally prescribed ceiling of $110 billion. The failure to come in under the ceiling occurred despite all the number-juggling and off-the-books spending. Under the automatic reductions, the Office of Management and Budget began withholding 4.3 percent of the Pentagon's funds and 5.3 percent of various other agencies' money, as well as 2 percent of Medicare payments made to hospitals and doctors.

A short while later, an agreement on how to bring down the deficit was reached—ridiculously, the deficit itself did not have to be lowered—and the cuts were quickly rescinded. So, toothless as it was, the law did little to encourage governmental frugality in Bush's early months. But it did provide yet another opportunity for political grandstanding about budgetary restraint. In October 1989, for example, two of its authors, Senator Phil Gramm of Texas and Senator Warren Rudman of New Hampshire, attributed several welcome developments in part to their bill. In a joint report, they noted that "average annual growth in federal spending has dropped from 4 percent in the years preceding Gramm-Rudman-Hollings to 1.6 percent since." They recalled that in the fall of 1988, when the Senate passed an amendment raising anti-drug funding by $3.2 billion, this expense "was fully offset with spending cuts in other areas." Earlier, they added, "the Senate killed a $1 billion farm credit bill on a point of order created" by their legislation. "Can anyone," they asked, imagine such things "happening before Gramm-Rudman-Hollings?"[7]

More significant than any of this was that almost two thirds of all federal spending, including pay of federal employees and Social Security payments, remained exempt from cuts mandated by the law, which also made no distinction between sound and unsound reductions. Had the reductions from the brief sequestration not been rescinded and remained in force for a full year, the Pentagon would have lost some 170,000 troops, seemingly a sensible cutback in light of easing East-West tensions. However, other would-be cutbacks would have been damaging: some $107 million from grants to states by the Environmental Protection Agency for sewage treatment plants, the loss of federal aid to about one million college students, and a 10 percent curtailment in work time for air-traffic controllers. That the sequestration provisions were implemented at all hardly represented a higher degree of fiscal responsibility in Washington, despite much rhetoric to the contrary. As Dan Rostenkowski, the Illinois Democrat, declared, "It's the sad truth that we have a president who refuses to lead and a Congress that is institutionally incapable of leading the deficit reduction effort." The sorry result, he said on the eve of the sequestration, "is Gramm-Rudman: Let the cuts go into effect [and] make them permanent and make them hurt"—which of course was not to happen.[8]

In early 1990, Rostenkowski again challenged Bush as well as many within the congressman's own Democratic party, this time to end "smoke-and-mirror" games and "feel-good promises" and take stronger steps to reduce the deficit. He proposed raising taxes on tobacco, alcohol, and gasoline, plus a higher federal tax rate on upper-income individuals whose top rate of 28 percent under the 1986 tax act was, perversely, 5 percentage points less than the maximum rate for people earning less. The congressman also proposed a 3 percent cut in the Pentagon's fiscal 1991 budget and a one-year freeze on cost-of-living increases for Social Security recipients. The various measures, he reckoned, would trim the federal deficit by about $512 billion over five years. He also proposed scrapping Gramm-Rudman, which he said was weak. Though the White House had encouraged the congressman to air his views—and they were largely sound ones, requiring political courage to declare—it did not follow through with leadership of its own once the proposal was made public, and this reluctance only increased when polls showed people generally to be opposed to much of the package.

A few years earlier, to be sure, no such proposals were emanating from any of Washington's leaders, Republican or Democrat; doubtless they would have been quickly rejected. But the reaction to Rostenkowski's plan, while hardly a joyous acceptance, did show at least a degree of receptivity unlikely in the Reagan years. House Budget Committee Chairman Panetta called it "a very positive contribution to the budget debate." Bob Dole, the Republican minority leader in the Senate, went even further, calling the plan "the wake-up call we've been waiting for." The proposal, he stated, "correctly challenged Congress, the administration, and the American people to face up to public enemy number one: the federal deficit."

In the main, however, serious efforts to reduce the deficit were undercut by the president's commitment not to raise taxes, which Rostenkowski's plan included. Just before the Gramm-Rudman sequestration move, the Democrat-led House produced a bill calling for what amounted to an array of tax boosts. These included a crackdown on tax refunds to companies generating big losses from leveraged buyouts, an increase in airport and airway taxes, repeal of special tax breaks for financial institutions aided in the S&L-bailout legislation, and a tax on ozone-depleting chemicals used, for example, in air conditioners. But the measures, which would have raised an estimated $5.4 billion, were unacceptable to Bush. Finally, in November, anxious to end the sequestration period, Congress approved a package of revenue-raising measures for fiscal 1990 that Bush readily endorsed. The measures— hardly bold moves—included raising $400 million by subjecting pay set aside in 401(k) retirement accounts to Social Security taxation and raising $895 million by delaying until 1991 scheduled cuts in taxes on airline tickets and doubling to $6 per passenger a charge on international tickets. Another provision hoped to raise $2.4 billion by requiring large employers to turn over faster to the Treasury the Social Security and income taxes withheld from paychecks.

Under increasing pressure, meantime, the Bush administration began taking a few modest, but well-publicized, steps to address mounting social problems. In November, the president called for $4.2 billion in federal funds, to be spent over three years, to help the rapidly growing number of homeless people and to promote homeownership among low-income people. The proposal—labeled HOPE for Homeownership for People Everywhere—also called for allowing first-time home buyers to use tax-sheltered Individual Retirement Accounts toward their down payments, without any penalty for early withdrawal.

However, the White House resisted larger moves, such as to restore greater progressivity to the tax system, which had grown increasingly regressive during Reagan's presidency. The Bush administration was unsympathetic, for example, to a proposal by New York Senator Daniel Moynihan to reduce the highly regressive Social Security payroll tax. With its flat rate and income cutoff level, the tax bears far more heavily on low- and middle-income taxpayers than on the wealthy, and it accounts for a steadily rising share of all federal revenues—close to 30 percent, up from 21 percent in the early 1980s. By his proposal, Moynihan hoped at least to draw attention to this regressivity, knowing full well that to adopt his plan would very likely force tax increases of a more progressive sort. The administration, responding as usual to its favored constituency, ignored Moynihan's proposal.

There were, in sum, scattered signs of headway against problems that for so long have eroded the economy's underpinnings. To face up fully to the challenge, however, demanded far bolder leadership than Washington was providing. And so, on balance, the erosion continued, with little prospect of a real change in course.

CHAPTER SIX

LOOKING AHEAD

Great nations have suffered decline, but they were imperial, or absolutist, or dominated by tradition-bound classes. Our nation is none of these. Our democracy holds the potential for resilience and rejuvenation in the face of any challenge. So ours is a winning hand.

—George P. Shultz, on January 9, 1989, in a speech
in Washington, at the end of his six and a half years
as secretary of state.

T H E   R O A D ahead will be rough. No nation has managed to live beyond its means indefinitely and still prosper, and there is no reason to assume that America will be the first. There still are no free lunches. The business cycle with its periodic downturns is alive and well.

As the downturn confronting Bush intensifies, the federal budget will sink deeper into deficit, as revenues diminish along with incomes and relief payments climb along with unemployment. With the overload of debt, bankruptcies—personal as well as corporate—will reach levels dwarfing the already high rates of Bush's early presidency. Capital spending, which typically keeps climbing in the early stages as a recession develops, will begin to decline as corporate profits, already dropping as 1990 began, fall further. With less corporate money for new plant and equipment, productivity will slow, eroding U.S. competitiveness and driving up labor costs as pay gains fail to be offset through higher output. As profitability weakens, the stock and bond markets will decline further and layoffs will spread. This in turn will depress consumer spending, which accounts for roughly two thirds of overall economic activity.

Such trends have always accompanied downturns of the business cycle, and there is no reason to assume they won't do so again. While the intensity may differ from one recession to the next, the degree of pain is normally greatest after long expansions—such as the one we have just experienced—in which there has been ample opportunity for excesses such as overborrowing to build up. Bush and Congress may wish to revoke the business cycle—at least its down phases—but this is not possible. The economy has always grown cyclically, with downturns following expansions as night does day, and there is no reason for the process not to continue.

In fact, the National Bureau of Economic Research in Cambridge, Massachusetts, has kept track of the ups and downs of the business cycle since 1854. In that time, the nonprofit research organization has detected thirty clear downturns of the cycle and thirty bona fide expansions. The downturns, on the average, have lasted eighteen months and the expansions thirty-three months. This enduring pattern of two steps forward and then one step back is how the economy has grown over the decades, though the length and intensity of individual phases of the cycle have varied greatly. The longest downturn, from 1879 to 1882, persisted sixty-five months, and the shortest, in 1980, lasted only six months. The longest expansion, from 1961 to 1969, lasted 106 months and the shortest, from 1919 to 1920, went on for only ten months.

Altogether, the record of nearly a century and a half of general business activity leaves little doubt that the business cycle is an enduring feature of the U.S. economic scene. Even so, some forecasters were pronouncing the business cycle dead around the time Bush became president. They believed that a new era of recession-free economic growth had finally dawned, talk that recalled the late 1960s, also a time of prolonged expansion. I recall, particularly, a monthly Commerce Department publication called *Business Cycle Developments* which tracked the ups and downs of the business cycle. The economy had expanded for nearly a decade when Lyndon Johnson's confident young economists became convinced that through judicious manipulation of fiscal and monetary policy—what they called fine-tuning—it was at last possible for Washington to perpetuate expansions. So they pronounced the business cycle dead and, among other foolish things, ordered that the title of the Commerce publication be changed from *Business Cycle Developments* to *Business Conditions Digest,* retaining only the *BCD* acronym. But no sooner was the change made than the economy entered the recession of 1969–70, and since then three more recessions have come and gone—1973–75, 1980, and 1981–82. Subsequent administrations did not see fit to change the name back to *Business Cycle Developments,* and in early 1990 Bush's economists halted the publication altogether—which suggests to me, if the late-1960s experience is any sort of omen, that the economy will now decline with a vengeance.

Whatever develops in the longer run, Washington in the near term faces an array of Hobson's choices. A recession seems unavoidable, and the excesses of the past decade suggest that before it can run its course, the economy must slump deeply. Turmoil in the oil-rich Middle East only increases the likelihood, fueling inflationary pressures which stifle bona fide growth. As joblessness spreads, increased payments to the newly unemployed should in theory help sustain buying power. But such payments would also tend to deepen the budget deficit, already ballooning on account of the Middle East, and thus increase the Treasury's already huge borrowing needs. And this would push up interest rates—hardly conducive to economic recovery. Cutting taxes is another traditional way to bolster buying power in a recession, but this too would increase Treasury borrowing and raise interest rates; as 1990 unfolded, taxes seemed likely to move up at the federal level and were already doing so at state and local government levels. In addition, the Federal Reserve could pump up the money supply to try to spur the economy, but this would weaken the already fragile dollar, worsen inflation, and make imports still costlier. Moreover, the prospect of a weakening dollar would discourage potential foreign lenders, further straining Treasury borrowing.

Some analysts claim, with the increased sophistication of computers, that inventory levels have kept in closer line with sales than in the past, which should prevent or at least lessen the severity of a new recession. These analysts contend that recessions usually have developed only when inventories became excessive and had to be worked down. But excessive inventories don't precipitate recessions. Rather, they tend to deepen recessions already under way. In any event, excessive debt can also weigh on economic activity, even if inventories are lean, and debt of all sorts has reached unprecedented heights. Nor is the increasingly important service sector a guarantee against a severe recession, though it's true that inventories play a relatively minor role in most service businesses.

R E C E S S I O N S do eventually end, and when they do the economy is normally cleansed of the excesses built up in the preceding period of expansion. This provides a base for renewed expansion. The recession before the long 1980s expansion, in 1981–82, was the worst downturn since the 1930s. In the course of the 1981–82 recession, inflation fell to less than 3 percent from above 10 percent, and there was a similar slowdown in the rise of unit labor costs. Meanwhile, the amount of consumer installment debt outstanding as a percentage of personal income fell to about 11 percent from 15 percent. Conversely, the shortest recession on record, a six-month downturn early in 1980, was followed by the shortest, weakest expansion in sixty years, an upturn lasting only twelve months. In the 1980 recession, inflation remained above 10 percent throughout the downturn and then rapidly increased in the ensuing business recovery. Labor costs actually rose during the recession, which was not the normal pattern, and consumer installment debt remained above 13 percent of income.

The options for policymakers now are limited. When the economy entered a severe recession in the early 1970s and another one in the early 1980s, oil was in short supply and its cost was rising sharply. As 1990 began, this was a fading memory. But Iraq's invasion of Kuwait changed all this. And even if oil in the years just ahead should remain plentiful and its price should be reasonably stable, most projections show a worsening shortage in the next century.

There are a few bright spots. The growing economic role of

service businesses, which now account for some three quarters of all jobs, provides a new element of stability. The service sector is less volatile than manufacturing, the fortunes of which depend more on keeping inventories in line. Service businesses may pay less and grow less swiftly in recoveries than manufacturing firms, whose inventories must be rebuilt quickly to meet reviving demand, but when slumps set in, services also hold up relatively well, while manufacturers must struggle to pare payrolls and inventories as orders drop.

The Federal Reserve, in addition, seems to be more adept at managing monetary policy. With the increasing sophistication and speed of the agency's computers, Fed officials can keep a closer tab on the economy's health. They receive important financial and economic data much sooner and in far greater detail than they did years ago. In early post–World War II years, the Fed was often flying blind, unable to measure inventory levels promptly in key industries or patterns of hiring and firing. Moreover, less was understood about the linkages between shifts in the money supply and the subsequent impact on economic activity. Confusion about this relationship often deepened economic downturns. After the stock market crash in October 1929, the Fed instead of easing money tightened it in a misguided effort to arrest a fall in interest rates. Between 1929 and 1933, the money supply fell by about a third, yet the decline in interest rates persisted and the worst slump in American history deepened.

After the stock market crash of October 1987, which was even sharper than the 1929 crash, the Fed pursued a very different course, even though interest rates once again were dropping. It eased money and ordered its member banks to make funds readily available to stock-brokerage firms and other financial outfits caught short by the market's plunge. Soon the economy steadied and the expansion continued, defying the forecasts of most economists that a recession would strike before the year was over.

Notwithstanding events in the Middle East, the easing of political tensions between the United States and the Soviet Union is a huge potential plus for policymakers. The budget deficit will increase when economic activity and revenues fall and unemployment and spending for the jobless rise. However, the deficit will increase less sharply if defense spending declines and the money saved is used at least in part to hold down the deficit. Defense cutbacks add to unemployment, at least in the short run, but the overall impact of this has been overstated. While some 3.2 million persons perform defense work at various corporations, fewer than 500,000 actually hold jobs not readily adaptable to civilian needs, such as producing bombs, tanks, warships or other weapons.[1] The great majority of defense workers turn out clothes, trucks, food, and other items that have extensive civilian markets as well as a military one. According to Labor Department analysts, fewer than 50,000 defense workers would lose their jobs annually in this decade, even if the Defense Department were to stop all weapons production—which of course will not happen. Within a total U.S. labor force of more than 125 million, 250,000 jobs over five years is not a devastating number.

This is not to say that reducing defense spending will be simple or painless, especially after Iraq's aggression. There was a foretaste of the difficulty of cutting back early in 1990 when a builder of reactors for nuclear submarines, UNC Naval Products, laid off 166 of its 1,060 workers and told the rest that they would also be let go over the next few years. The dismissals, all in the New London area of Connecticut, resulted from a Pentagon decision to cut back output of the Navy's fast-attack class of submarine, intended mainly to hunt down and destroy Soviet missile submarines in the event of a war between the two superpowers. UNC workers staged a rally in April in Montville, Connecticut, to protest the cutbacks. Three area congressmen and Connecticut Senator Christopher J. Dodd attended and promised to seek legislation to ease the workers' transition to nondefense jobs. The legislators also assured the rally that they would urge the Department of Energy to steer nonmilitary projects to UNC. Beyond the promises, however, little else was achieved, and the unemployment in the area continued to rise. The company, meantime, set up a job-counseling program for the furloughed workers.

Another foretaste of readjustment problems occurred slightly earlier at Grumman Corp., among the nation's ten largest defense contractors and the largest employer of any sort on Long Island. Grumman's products for the military included the Navy's A-6 attack bomber, which the Navy had planned to refit, but then, in early 1989, it canceled the plan. Grumman then dismissed about 2,500 workers. With these firings, plus earlier ones caused by other Pentagon cutbacks, Grumman's work force by early 1990 had shrunk by 7,200, to less than 18,000. The company also offered early-retirement packages to an additional 6,000 employees. By midyear, many of the laid-off workers were still jobless, and those who had managed to find new work were often earning substantially less pay than they had received with Grumman. One such worker had traded a $42,800-a-year engineering job at Grumman for a $30,000 job designing exhibits for trade shows. To help the sixty-year-old manage the job change, Grumman paid some $6,000 for him to attend a 1,000-hour retraining program where he studied drafting techniques helpful in the trade-show work.[2]

Meanwhile, demographic trends are beginning to encourage a healthier pattern of saving and investing. Mindful of their children's rapidly increasing college costs and their own eventual retirements, people normally try to save more and borrow less as they get older. As they gain experience and grow more valuable in their jobs, they also tend to earn more. By 1990, the postwar baby boomers, whose ages ranged from twenty-five to forty-three years, were entering the years of high savings and high earnings in rapidly rising numbers. Citing this, some economists forecast that the savings rate will move above 10 percent within a few years.[3] In fact, savings in 1990 were near 5 percent of after-tax income, more than twice the rate in some months of Reagan's presidency, which was marked by excessive spending. After the 1981–82 recession, America's approximately 90 million households went on an unprecedented spending spree for the rest of the decade. They bought 62 million microwave ovens, 57 million washers and dryers, 88 million automobiles and light trucks, 105 million color TV sets, 46 million refrigerators and freezers, 63 million VCRs, 31 million cordless telephones, and 30 million telephone-answering machines. Overall consumer spending, including service outlays, rose to about 66 percent of the gross national product in those years, up from a 63 percent average for the first three postwar decades.

In the same period, it should be added, military spending also climbed sharply. Near the end of Reagan's presidency, after a prolonged and controversial military buildup, the U.S. armed forces numbered nearly 2,200,000 on active duty, with another 1,638,000 in the ready reserves. As a share of the gross national product, defense spending in the United States came to about 7 percent, compared to rates of only 3.3 percent for the European Community as a whole, 1.6 percent in Japan, and less than 5 percent in China. Among the major nations, only Russia, with its defense outlays at roughly 20 percent of its GNP, had devoted more attention to its military. In per capita terms, the United States was spending $1,164 on its military effort, compared with $454 in West Germany and only $163 in Japan. Moreover, some 70 percent of the American research-and-development effort was defense-related, against 12.5 percent in West Germany and only 4.5 percent in Japan. In all, we spent $1.8 trillion on defense during Reagan's eight years, and there is no question that this huge outlay contributed mightily to the federal budget deficit and other economic worries. As the Capitol Steps, a Washington theatrical group, put it in a 1989 musical spoof about the causes of the budget deficit, "immense expense is mainly in defense"—sung, of course, to the tune of the rain-in-Spain song from *My Fair Lady*.

P O L I C Y M A K E R S must grapple as best they can with unemployment and other near-term recessionary problems. But they must also find ways to make the economy sound for the longer haul, and to achieve this they must begin to reduce the federal deficit and redirect federal spending to enhance productivity; for example, by investing in infrastructure improvements. However, the reduction must be carried out with great care, so as not to cripple an already slowing economy. Federal taxes should be raised cautiously but unmistakably, not in a fashion to be confused with "revenue enhancement." This surely would not cripple the economy. After all, compared to taxation in other countries, the American tax burden is relatively light. At about 29 percent of overall output, the tax rate in the United States is far less onerous, for instance, than in France, where the comparable rate is 45 percent, or in Britain or West Germany, where it is 38 percent, or in Italy, where it is 36 percent, or in Canada, where it is 33 percent.

There is no shortage of sensible ways to raise taxes, and this becomes more palatable with the easing of East-West tensions; revenues are likelier to be used for tackling domestic ills rather than for still more weapons for the Cold War. A Congressional Budget Office study, issued barely a month after Bush's inauguration—but largely ignored by the White House—contained four hundred pages of revenue-raising options.[4] While some may be dismissed as unsound or politically impossible, many are reasonable and, with stronger leadership in Washington, could have been adopted early on. For perspective, individual income taxes in 1989 produced about 45 percent of overall federal revenue, Social Security taxes produced 36 percent, and corporate income taxes produced 10 percent. The remaining 9 percent of revenue was generated through customs duties and other charges. Estate and gift taxes contributed a mere 1 percent to the total.

To increase revenue and reduce the deficit, a huge sum—an estimated $94 billion over five years—could be raised, according to the CBO, simply by increasing the top marginal income-tax rate to 30 percent from 28 percent, along the lines that Dan Rostenkowski had already proposed. Eliminating the deductibility of state and local tax payments would generate an estimated $126.2 billion over the same period. A 5 percent federal sales tax—excepting such essentials as food, housing, and medical care—would produce an estimated $281.9 billion over five years. And a 12-cents-a-gallon increase in motor-fuel taxes would yield some $57.8 billion. About 25 percent of the retail price of gasoline in the United States, on the average, represents federal and state levies, compared to rates as high as 67 percent in Britain, 77 percent in France, 78 percent in Italy, 46 percent in Japan, 39 percent in Canada, and 63 percent in West Germany. Not surprisingly, the price of gasoline abroad is also far higher than in the United States, but cars crowd the highways nonetheless.

Taxing credit unions on the same basis as other thrift institutions would produce an additional $3.5 billion; there is no sound reason not to do so. Reducing deductions for the cost of business meals and entertainment to 50 percent from 80 percent would add $15.5 billion. Whatever legitimate business is conducted as a result of this tax break can just as well be carried out by phone or in the office. The rule is largely a result of intense congressional lobbying by restaurant and hotel lobbyists and should be scrapped. Raising the tax rate on beer and wine to the same level as for hard liquor would generate $24.2 billion. Taxes on hard liquor and cigarettes, as well as on beer and wine, have risen far less than the general price level over the years. Had the federal excise tax on a fifth of liquor kept pace with inflation over the last couple of decades, it would be above $5 per bottle instead of just under $2.

The CBO's list of revenue-raising options is but one of many such compilations to be assembled in and out of Washington in Bush's early months, and while the specific proposals vary from one study to the next, the thrust is that tax increases are essential to narrowing the budget deficit.

The government should also charge more for many services that benefit only a limited number of people, often wealthy people. Some $1.8 billion could be raised between 1991 and 1995 by imposing user fees on the nation's system of inland waterways, according to the CBO estimates. Charging for various Coast Guard services would generate another $3.8 billion. In 1990, the Army Corps of Engineers spent over $300 million to maintain and operate the waterway system, and all of this was paid for by general taxpayers. Fairness dictates that waterway users, many of whom are well-to-do boat owners, should pay. Similarly, individuals or particular businesses that directly benefit from the activities of the Coast Guard, such as its search-and-rescue operations and marine-safety instruction, should pay more. The money raised could be redirected to such broader Coast Guard duties as drug interdiction and enforcing coastal fishing laws. The same applies for the Corps of Engineers. Some years ago, a friend with marshy property along the waterway system in eastern Long Island was actually paid a small sum by the government to allow the Corps of Engineers to dump dredged fill on his land. He was delighted, for when the fill had settled the land was no longer tidal and he was able to develop and sell it. Today, several expensive vacation homes occupy the raised land. The government had paid my friend for enriching himself.

Taxes can be increased in ways that offer benefits beyond simply paring the deficit. They can be raised so as to induce Americans to save and invest more and spend and borrow less, coaxing investments more into new plant and equipment and less into housing, and promoting a more even distribution of wealth and income. A sales-type tax would encourage saving and discourage consumption, and the rate need not be as high as the 5 percent suggested by the CBO. The regressive aspects of such a tax could be lessened by exempting goods and services, such as food and shelter, which bulk large in the budgets of low-income households. A tighter limit on home-mortgage deductions, beyond the modest constraints of the 1986 tax act, would not only generate revenue but channel funds from housing into production facilities, which are sorely needed. Some $8 billion could be generated over five years by capping deductions of home-mortgage interest at $20,000 per joint tax return and at $12,000 per individual return. Housing lobbyists would rebel, of course, but firm leadership in Washington could overcome that.

After the increasing concentration of the Reagan years, a tax on capital gains at death would not only raise revenue but bring about a more equitable wealth distribution. Another move in the right direction would be to lower the exemption ceiling on estate and gift taxes, which under Reagan was foolishly raised to $600,000. Lowering it to, say, $225,000 would generate an estimated $15 billion over five years. Through tax breaks provided during Reagan's presidency, the number of estates subject to taxation dropped by about two thirds. The 1981 tax act more than tripled—to $600,000 from $175,625—the sum that an individual may leave tax-free to an heir. Accordingly, only 3 percent of estates now are taxed, down from about 10 percent before Reagan. For very large estates still subject to tax, the highest marginal rate was cut to 55 percent from 70 percent.

To take the ceiling off the Social Security tax would also make the tax system more fair. The present arrangement clearly favors the relatively well-off, since the same 7.65 percent is assessed from all paychecks up to a wage ceiling of $50,000. So the more a person earns above $50,000 each year, the lower will be the share of income collected for Social Security. By eliminating this cutoff, the Social Security tax rate for everyone, employers as well as employees, could be cut by more than 2 percentage points, without reducing the system's receipts.

. . .

C U T T I N G the budget deficit will also require reduced
federal spending, which should be less difficult politically than
raising taxes. For one thing, Bush would not be eating his words,
as he was finally forced to do on the tax front in mid-1990. More
important, the range of targets is enormous and the spending cuts
could be made by and large where the recipients of federal hand-
outs are least in need. The agricultural sector, a beneficiary of
price and income supports totaling some $25 billion in 1988–89, is
a good candidate. Hollywood makes money at the box office
portraying farmers as downtrodden and strapped, but the average farm family's income was above the average for the country
as a whole throughout the 1980s, and the average farm family's
net worth exceeds the national average. For the 1980s as a whole,
taxpayers and consumers paid more than $250 billion to support
U.S. farmers. Yet, according to a 1990 study by the Cato Institute
in Washington, "there is nothing to show for these outlays except
idled acres, polluted groundwater, and richer farmers." By the
CBO's estimate, some $2 billion could be saved over five years
simply by cutting farm-support payments to a maximum of
$50,000 per year per participant, down from the prevailing
$100,000 limit that only the largest, most prosperous farm opera-
tors normally reach. In 1988, about 43 percent of federal farm aid
went to farmers whose incomes averaged $96,000 and whose net
worth averaged $804,000. Even so, in July 1990 Congress passed
bills tending to perpetuate this sorry situation. With Iraq's invasion of Kuwait, it should be added, the government's fiscal 1991
farm costs took another $1 billion leap, as loans to support farm
exports to Iraq became worthless.

Another ready target is the vast entitlements area, where, as
with agriculture, huge federal sums wind up in the hands of many
well-off individuals. Some 85 percent of the more than $500 billion
in entitlement outlays is for programs in which no means test is
required. Much of this money is earmarked for the elderly, who,
as a group, collect close to 30 percent of all federal outlays, even
though only 12 percent of the population are over sixty-five years
old. For perspective, education commands less than 3 percent of

total spending, yet nearly 40 percent of the population are under twenty-five.

A tougher government attitude toward non-means-tested entitlements would save many billions of dollars. Current federal law requires no waiting period before jobless workers may receive unemployment insurance. If a two-week waiting period were required, federal outlays would be reduced by an estimated $1.2 billion annually. This would not alter the ultimate amount of jobless benefits unemployed workers would get, which is normally twenty-six weeks' worth. But such a move might well discourage the aimless job-hopping that Labor Department analysts say accounts for a large, rising part of overall unemployment.

If the cost-of-living adjustment for Social Security beneficiaries were held to two-thirds the increase in the consumer price index, the saving would approximate $52 billion over five years. Applying the same formula to other non-means-tested programs would save an additional $13.9 billion. As Rostenkowski found when he proposed curbing cost-of-living adjustments, any such move is bound to encounter stiff opposition from lobbyists for the elderly. It would require stronger leadership than Washington in the past has shown. But the case can be made that a limited adjustment for inflation, while painful, would ultimately lead to a healthier economy, which would benefit the elderly as well as other Americans.

There is even room to trim some programs aimed at young people. The National School Lunch Program pays schools to feed not only children of poor households but children who are relatively well-off. Cutting reimbursements for the well-off children would save the government some $2.2 billion over five years. Another $900 million could be saved by eliminating federal subsidies to students preparing for careers in health care, mainly as physicians. Since physicians earn, on the average, over $120,000 a year, students seeking to be physicians would presumably have little difficulty financing their educations privately, borrowing if necessary against future income. A doctor shortage might require subsidies, but there is none. In a recent fifteen-year period, the number of physicians per 100,000 people in the United States rose from 161 to 228.

Opportunities to cut spending are numerous. An estimated $1.2

billion could be saved between 1991 and 1995 by closing down the Export-Import Bank. The Washington-based agency attempts to boost U.S. exports by providing cheap credit to foreign buyers of U.S.-made goods. Most of this aid is for purchases of items that already have healthy order backlogs, such as passenger jets. For instance, airplane-related business accounted for about 75 percent of the Ex-Im Bank's credit in 1987. Such financing is a hidden subsidy for large U.S. corporations fully capable of fending for themselves.

Ending loans and loan guarantees by the Small Business Administration would save about $2 billion over five years. Through the SBA, the government guarantees 90 percent of the principal for business loans of up to $155,000 and from 70 percent to 85 percent for loans over $155,000. The agency also lends directly, generally up to $150,000, to businesses in areas of high unemployment or low income, as well as to businesses owned by minorities, handicapped people, and Vietnam veterans. SBA assistance naturally gravitates to firms rejected by conventional lenders, the businesses least likely to generate jobs and enhance productivity and competitiveness. The SBA program may be well-intentioned, but it is largely ineffective and too costly. Moreover, as we have seen, the SBA itself is poorly managed.

A sterner line should be taken with Third World recipients of U.S. largess whose richest citizens perennially manage to deposit much of their personal wealth elsewhere than at home. An estimated $12 billion left Brazil illegally in 1989, up from $7.5 billion the year before. Yet Brazil owed foreigners, mainly the United States, some $120 billion, and it remains doubtful that much of this will ever be repaid. Morgan Guaranty Trust has estimated that Brazilian "flight capital" held abroad exceeds $31 billion, and even this vast sum is less than the comparable amounts for Mexico ($84 billion), Venezuela ($58 billion), and Argentina ($46 billion). It is high time that either such hemorrhaging be stopped from within or aid from without be sharply curtailed.

It is also time, with the Cold War over, that wherever possible foreign aid of a largely military nature be sharply curtailed. The largest recipient by far is Israel, which receives some $3 billion in aid from the United States each year. With such Soviet clients in the Middle East as Syria receiving far less aid from the USSR and Eastern Europe, there is no reason for the United States not to cut back as well. But to do so would once again require political courage. When Senate Minority Leader Robert Dole called in early 1990 for a modest 5 percent cut in U.S. aid to Israel and some other long-standing recipients, as well as a modest boost in aid to Eastern Europe, even his Republican colleagues in Congress were critical and the White House wanted nothing to do with the idea.

Looking beyond the turmoil in the Middle East, with improved East-West relations the defense sector offers large cost-cutting opportunities. Even before the end of the Berlin Wall and the Malta summit in late 1989, plans were afoot to rein in military spending. Soon after Bush took office, the CBO produced a long list of possible defense cuts. Canceling further development and procurement of the F-14 Air Force fighter plane would save an estimated $7.2 billion over five years. Slowing procurement of the C-17 transport aircraft would save $4.8 billion, and slowing procurement of DDG-51 guided-missile destroyers would save $7.3 billion. Delaying or canceling production of the B-2 Stealth bomber would save some $68 billion. Slowing work on the Strategic Defense Initiative, better known as Star Wars, would save $17.6 billion. Reducing the number of deployable aircraft carriers to thirteen from the fifteen planned under Reagan would trim $4.8 billion. Persuading allies to pay more of the cost of stationing U.S. forces abroad—apart from the Middle East emergency—would save $17.1 billion.

Some 60 percent of the Pentagon's budget in recent years has gone toward the defense of Western Europe, and the United States has spent more on the North Atlantic Treaty Organization than the other members combined. NATO has amounted to "a virtual entitlement program" for America's allies, and to support it has forced the United States to "tolerate huge trade imbalances and struggle with an unbearable federal deficit," says Andy Ireland, a Republican congressman from Florida. "American tax dollars are spent to defend our allies who use the money they save to clobber us in the trade wars."[5]

The "peace dividend" from an end to the Cold War—estimated by many analysts to reach as high as $150 billion annually late in this decade—could help reduce the budget deficit as well as finance such urgent domestic needs as education, health care, repair of infrastructure, and environmental cleanup, challenges that could gobble up $150 billion a year several times over. But the peace dividend is sinking in the Persian Gulf. Moreover, the budget situation as Bush took office was very different from two decades earlier, when there was talk of a "peace dividend" from winding down the Vietnam War. The budget was in surplus then, but even so the supposed peace dividend of some $40 billion a year was soon consumed by accelerating inflation and sharp spending increases at virtually every federal agency. Among other things, Congress indexed Social Security benefits to inflation and greatly expanded such costly programs as Medicare and Medicaid. Of course, the Cold War was still in progress, so even with peace in Vietnam, strategic defense spending, a huge expense, kept rising. This is unlikely in the wake of Malta.

A few statistics underscore the impact of past defense spending on domestic needs. From 1978 to 1983, after adjusting for inflation, military spending rose 28 percent, while federal grants-in-aid to states and localities dropped 25 percent. These grants were used, for example, to help local governments maintain bridges and roads, mass transit, prisons, and waste-disposal facilities.

Despite much reluctance in the White House and Congress, it is encouraging that in 1990 the Bush administration became increasingly serious about reducing defense costs. Finally, after weeks of congressional pressure, Defense Secretary Dick Cheney on April 26 proposed to cut back sharply the planned production of the B-2 Stealth bomber and several other types of expensive military aircraft. "We can afford to slow down the pace of developing and fielding our next generation of aircraft," he told Congress. He proposed, among other reductions, cutting the number of B-2s to 75 from 132, the number of C-17 long-range transports to 120 from 210, and the number of A-12 advanced tactical fighter aircraft to 620 from 858. The potential saving works out to $35 billion.

Senate Armed Services Committee Chairman Sam Nunn welcomed Cheney's package as "a more sensible approach." Earlier, the powerful Georgia Democrat had complained that the Pentagon had a considerable "ways to go" to reduce its expenditures.

Cheney also indicated plans to reduce the number of aircraft carriers to twelve, abandoning the fifteen-carrier force that was central to Reagan's buildup program for the Navy. A few days later, on May 1, Cheney extended a freeze on all military construction projects and suggested that 207 of the projects be scrapped entirely.

For all of this, pressure for larger cutbacks continued to mount. Senator Nunn called for a further reduction of some $7 billion in the $295 billion in military spending that Cheney proposed for 1991. Nunn urged the complete elimination of the Pentagon's plans for new Seawolf-type fast-attack submarines, A-12 aircraft, and advanced air-to-air missiles. By the year 2000, according to Navy planning, the fleet would have ten Seawolf submarines, at a projected cost of over $1 billion each. Nunn also challenged the Bush administration's view that 195,000 troops in Central Europe constituted a floor below which the United States could not prudently go. "We must begin planning for a significantly lower level" of 75,000 to 100,000 within five years, the senator declared.

Anticipating troop cutbacks in Europe, the Army, with some 760,000 personnel, had already reduced the size of its recruiting classes to 92,000 a year from 120,000 and cut its 1990 advertising budget to $60 million, which was $3 million less than in 1989 and nearly $20 million less than in the last years of Reagan's presidency. Secretary of the Army Michael Stone had also conceded that as many as 250,000 soldiers could safely be cut from the ranks by the middle of the decade. And on the heels of Nunn's call for cutbacks, General Colin L. Powell, the chairman of the Joint Chiefs of Staff, called for a hard look at "every single hardware system" in the armed forces, as well as a review of personnel levels, training practices, and military bases. The upshot, according to Powell, could well be a 25 percent reduction in the Pentagon's budget over five years, which would be a considerably sharper retrenchment than the 2 percent a year cut proposed a short while before by Defense Secretary Cheney. To achieve the goal, of course, would require a lasting settlement in the Middle East.

The political feasibility of the various proposals to raise taxes and trim spending varies, of course, from one measure to the next. In May 1990, a poll asked how, if taxes had to be raised and

spending cut, this might best be done. Eighty percent urged raising taxes on beer and liquor and 78 percent urged a higher tax rate
on incomes over $200,000. But only 40 percent supported a higher
gasoline tax and only 30 percent approved setting up a federal
sales tax. On the matter of spending, 83 percent urged a cut in
foreign aid, while 64 percent supported military cutbacks. But
only 20 percent endorsed reduced spending on the environment,
only 16 percent urged a curb on Social Security outlays, and only
12 percent endorsed less aid to education.[6]

G R A M M - R U D M A N - H O L L I N G S   could
be toughened by counting more off-budget spending in calculating
whether the law's deficit targets are met. Social Security reserves, supposedly for the baby-boomer retirement wave but actually being spent, should not count toward compliance. A
tougher version of Gramm-Rudman-Hollings could be part of a
revised budget law, replacing the inadequate act of 1974. Since
then, federal spending has more than tripled. Among the act's
mistakes was to take away the impoundment power that presi-
dents once used to counter congressional overspending. This
power should be reinstituted.

Congress also should give the president the authority to exer-
cise so-called line-item vetoes, which Bush has sought. Line-item
veto power would permit the president to eliminate or reduce in
surgical fashion parts of big appropriations bills; now the president is forced to approve or veto entire bills. Congress could still
override such vetoes through a two-thirds majority vote. Bush has
suggested there may be a basis in the Constitution for a presidential line-item veto, but few legal scholars agree. Every recent
president has sought the line-item veto, but Congress has been
unwilling to go along. So spending bills as long as two thousand
pages wind up in the Oval Office for the presidential signature,
though no member of Congress or the president could possibly
read them through. When Bush took office, forty-three governors
had line-item-veto power over their state budgets, and the growth
of spending in those states has been appreciably slower than in
states without line-item vetoes. The economist Milton Friedman
has proposed that if Congress continues to bar the line-item veto,

it should at least forbid any spending bill longer than the Constitution, which contains about 7,500 words.

A variation of the line-item idea, perhaps more palatable to Congress, is enhanced recision. This would allow the president to disapprove, at least temporarily, individual parts of spending measures, and then let Congress vote on his action. Attempting to mandate a balanced budget through an amendment to the Constitution enjoys considerable support, particularly among conservatives, but this seems out of touch with economic realities. The economy is subject to periodic expansions and recessions, as we have seen, and these cyclical swings exert a great impact on the budget. To try to balance it during, say, a deep recession would be impossible. By the same token, the budget should be in surplus, not merely balanced, when the economy is enjoying a sustained expansion, though this was not the case during the long expansion of the 1980s.

A smaller budget deficit would help reduce the trade deficit. Through the budget deficit, Americans have lived beyond their means, spending and consuming more than they have managed to produce and sell, and the trade deficit reflects this shortfall. Goods from abroad have served to forestall a far sharper decline in living standards than has so far occurred. But the trade deficit, in turn, has been financed through inflows of foreign capital, transforming the United States into the world's largest debtor. C. Fred Bergsten, director of the Institute for International Economics, stressed this linkage in testimony before Congress in early 1989. "We do not need a recession to cure our trade imbalance," he said, adding that simply "to eliminate the budget deficit" would do the job.[7] A smaller budget deficit would reduce the Treasury's need to borrow, which would help lower interest rates and free funds to invest more in productive facilities and less in simply helping the Treasury roll over its debt. This in turn would serve to improve U.S. competitiveness and thus strengthen the nation's trade balance.

Cutting the budget deficit would also help increase savings, as a healthier economy attracts more investment. It is no accident that the countries saving most also have shown the best economic growth. In the 1980s, Japan saved more than 30 percent of its total economic output and West Germany saved 22 percent, while the U.S. rate of 16 percent was the lowest among seven leading industrial countries.

Other measures could help raise the U.S. savings level. The deduction for individual retirement accounts, which was unwisely cut back during Reagan's presidency, should be reinstituted and expanded. IRAs were created in 1974, under the Employee Retirement Income Security Act, which allowed individuals not covered by employer-sponsored retirement plans to set aside $1,500 a year. At the start of the 1980s, this was raised to $2,000 and made applicable to all taxpayers. But the Tax Reform Act of 1986 restricted IRA deductions once again to people not covered by employer-sponsored plans or with low incomes. This was done supposedly to save the government $12 billion annually in lost tax revenues, but in the previous five years IRAs had added an estimated $138 billion to savings, so the trade-off was poor. Claims that to expand IRA deductions would help only the rich are simply untrue. About one fifth of the $138 billion was from taxpayers earning less than $25,000 a year, and over four fifths was from those with incomes under $75,000. Sensibly, the Bush administration has sought to replace the scaled-down IRA program with a broader plan aimed at middle-income households.

Cutting the tax rate on capital gains would also raise the incentive to save, making it more attractive for investors to put money into assets offering the potential for long-term growth, such as a fledgling manufacturing company that pays no dividend but promises, with a bit of luck, to grow and prosper. A reduced capital-gains rate would also encourage investors to realize more of their gains, which in turn would free funds for new, struggling enterprises. The Tax Reform Act of 1986 raised the top rate for capital gains to 33 percent from 20 percent, giving the United States the highest long-term-capital-gains rate of any major industrial nation. When state and local taxes are considered, the rate is even higher. A resident of New York City pays a capital-gains rate of close to 40 percent.

The impact of a reduced capital-gains rate on the budget is unclear. A lower rate would presumably increase revenues, as assets previously held off the market on account of the potential tax bite are unloaded. But some economists warn that as such selling diminishes in future years, the reduced gains rate would mean lower revenues. This is worrisome, but the spur that a lower rate would give to investment should outweigh the risk of reduced revenues down the road.

A sensible move unlikely to cause serious revenue loss would be to index gains to inflation, providing generous allowances on sales of long-held assets but raising the rate on sales of clearly speculative investments held only a short time. Cutting capital-gains taxation may on balance favor wealthy investors, as critics of such a move charge. At the same time, however, increasing the rate on short-term gains would especially hit wealthy investors, since they are most likely to speculate.

A further incentive to save and invest would be to eliminate the favorable tax treatment that debt gets over equity. A 1989 study found that "firms with large amounts of debt in their capital structure are committed to distributing a higher fraction of their earnings," rather than plowing them into new facilities, and this "spurred consumption" at the expense of savings.[8] A reasonable step would be to replace the interest deduction for corporations' debt expenses with a general deduction for both debt and equity costs such as dividends. Unlike other schemes that would simply reduce equity costs and thus deepen the budget deficit, this move could be arranged so as not to affect the Treasury's overall revenues.

An additional step to discourage corporations from piling up debt would be to toughen U.S. bankruptcy laws, which are far more lenient than those of most other countries. Capitalism without painful bankruptcy has been likened to Christianity without hell. In the United States, bankruptcy filings have resulted in frivolous use of the rules. Frank Lorenzo took Eastern Air Lines into bankruptcy to break a union. Raymond Hay took LTV into bankruptcy partly to unload the steel producer's pension liabilities of some $2.3 billion on a federal agency, the Pension Benefit and Guaranty Corp. At the least, bankruptcy regulations should be toughened so that the courts replace executives of firms filing for protection.

The greatly reduced risk of a nuclear conflict between the United States and Russia should also increase incentives to save and invest. Joel Slemrod, a University of Michigan economist, has found that in the United States, more than elsewhere, savings have been held down by widespread worry over nuclear annihilation. Why save if there is no future? Why not borrow and spend heavily and enjoy life? Over the postwar decades, according to Slemrod, the U.S. saving rate has generally risen in periods of eased U.S.-Soviet tension.

A greater effort must be made to attract able people to Washington. Paul Volcker, the former Federal Reserve chairman, has correctly warned that the government is "handicapped in carrying out programs by a weak civil service," which was allowed to deteriorate under Reagan. To rebuild it will necessitate, among other things, substantial federal pay increases. Only 16 percent of those receiving master's degrees from Harvard's Kennedy School of Government in the past decade have gone on to work for the federal government. Only one of 365 Yale seniors in a 1988 survey expressed an interest in a career in civil service. At the same time, more than 3,000 U.S. government jobs were political appointments, compared to only 60 in West Germany, 150 in Britain, and 400 in France. Recent proposals in Congress to set up incentives for young people to help provide public social services, such as aiding the homeless, are a small step in the right direction.

Congressional operations also need an overhaul. The ability of Congress to function has diminished as its bureaucracy has expanded. Each House member now has eighteen staff aides working full-time, and many senators have twice that number. There are forty-seven congressional committees, plus 244 subcommittees, all amply staffed. Altogether, Congress provides jobs for some 37,600 people. Of these, 7,400 are full-time Senate staffers and 19,500 are full-time employees on the House's payroll, while the rest are employed by various legislative agencies that work with Congress, such as the Congressional Budget Office. The salaries of these personnel range as high as $90,000. With a $222 million increase in 1990, the administrative budget of Congress exceeds $2.3 billion a year. Even so, the legislators increasingly seem inept at dealing with such challenges as the budget deficit, inadequate health care, lagging investment, a deteriorating infrastructure, and pollution of the environment. A poll in early 1990 found that only 15 percent of Americans had a high level of confidence in Congress, down from 24 percent in 1984.[9]

To make Congress more efficient, a first step would be to scale back its bureaucracy, perhaps halving the number of staffers allowed each legislator. A second step would be to ensure a greater turnover. Some 98 percent of House members are routinely reelected. A major reason involves so-called political action committees, money-raising organizations that represent powerful special interests. In the election year of 1988, PACs gave $115 million to incumbents in Congress and only $17 million to challengers. This imbalance is no small consideration when the expense of the average congressional campaign stands at about $380,000, with the increasingly important televisions about five times costlier than in 1976. To bring fresh blood to Congress, seven in ten Americans favor limiting by law the number of years a legislator may serve, much as the presidency is limited; the preferred cutoff for both representatives and senators is twelve years.[10] A less rigid, and in my view preferable, move would be to reduce sharply the amount of money that any candidate may receive. Under present law, a PAC may give a candidate up to $5,000 per election, but there is no cap on the total amount of PAC funds that a candidate may accept. A reasonable ceiling would be $75,000, with perhaps a slightly higher limit for candidates running in heavily populated districts. Better still would be to eliminate PACs altogether and institute a system of mandatory public campaign funding through the tax system. Another sound step would be to deny legislators subsidized postage in election years. It is encouraging that proposals to reform the system were initiated in both the Senate and the House in 1990.

A M E R I C A can no longer afford to live beyond its means. Bush's decision to pour military resources into the Middle East only makes this inability more pronounced. It is extraordinarily good fortune that a transformation has swept Eastern Europe and the Soviet Union which now permits America to shift some resources from the Cold War to domestic needs. However much it strained the Treasury, Reagan's determination to strengthen the military may have hastened this great political change, but a deeper reason must be the absurdity of a social and economic system rooted in the discredited theories of an eccentric nineteenth-century German political philosopher.

Before the Middle East upheaval, there were scattered signs that a start had been made to set things right—tenuous, to be sure, and marked by backsliding and intransigence. In early May of 1990, Bush held a Sunday-night meeting at the White House with the four top congressional leaders to launch talks on how to cut spending and—despite his pledge—raise taxes. Hoping to reduce the budget deficit, Bush told the lawmakers, at last, that "everything is on the table." Around the same time, Treasury officials began work to strengthen the nation's shaky financial structure. The plans included eliminating the tottering S&L industry by folding it into commercial banking, strengthening and streamlining the mazelike, overlapping system of financial regulation, and injecting an element of risk into federal deposit insurance by establishing a link between the amount of insurance guaranteed on each deposit and how deposited funds are invested; the riskier, higher-yielding investments would warrant smaller federal guarantees for depositors. The urgency of the problem was underscored in late May, when Treasury Secretary Brady asked Congress for massive new borrowing authority for the S&L bailout. He forecast that some one thousand S&Ls—40 percent of the industry—would eventually fail and that the $73 billion which Congress had already appropriated for the bailout was inadequate. He estimated that at least $89 billion and possibly as much as $130 billion would be needed.

With such burdens to be faced—the Middle East had not yet erupted—the 1990s hardly seemed likely to develop into "the most prosperous decade yet" for the United States, as *Business Week* magazine has forecast.[11] But America at least seemed to be *attempting*, however gingerly, to regain competitive stature through the neglected avenues of hard work and sacrifice.

This is by no means an impossible mission. There is a tendency among Americans, for example, to overrate the Japanese. We tend to overlook intrinsic advantages that the United States has over Japan. America's acreage of arable land is roughly thirty times that of Japan, and the United States has 1,300 times Japan's oil reserves and about 330 times its deposits of coal. There may also be a tendency to underrate what Americans can do if only they apply themselves. It is what the Japanese somewhat enviously call *sokojikara*—a resiliency and a capacity to recover from adversity in new, enterprising ways.

To present a perhaps extreme example, I recall a visit I paid one summer years ago to London, where I was briefly assigned for an American newspaper. I came to detect a correlation between the state of the London weather and absenteeism among the young English office assistants employed at the bureau. Health problems that precluded their working seemed invariably to arise on days when the weather was warm and sunny, but on damp and dreary days, which were the rule that summer, health difficulties remarkably disappeared and the bureau was fully staffed. Only slowly did I come to understand the attitude behind this malingering, a conviction that advancement to a higher station, at our office or at any other place of work in Britain, was never to be achieved: once an office clerk, always an office clerk. Christopher Lewinton, who served at that time as the managing director of Wilkinson Sword Ltd., the razor-blade maker, explained why such relatively low-level British workers seemed less industrious than their U.S. counterparts. The British executive, who had spent much of his career in the United States as chief of Wilkinson's American operations, said, "You Americans don't have to cope with the problems of a class system, as we British employers do." Lewinton went on to explain that a new employee in a British company, because of his social background, all too often comes to work with the resigned attitude that rigid limits will govern how high he can ever rise within the firm. "In the States," Lewinton recalled, "even the lowliest office clerk often has the idea, which is sometimes correct, that he can someday reach a much higher job level. As a result, he is generally willing to work harder than his British counterpart."

There seems as well to be a tendency among Americans to view some pressing U.S. problems in isolation, without regard to what may be occurring elsewhere. There is no question that environmental pollution poses a severe challenge that Bush has largely failed to address. Yet a Conference Board report on air quality, for instance, shows not a single American city listed among the world's two hundred cities with the highest levels of sulfur dioxide. In fact, sulfur dioxide emissions in the United States declined about 35 percent in a recent ten-year period, while concentrations of airborne lead dropped 88 percent. In the period, U.S. utility companies installed 149 scrubbers, which removed some 90 percent of the sulfur dioxide from stack emissions. Meanwhile, automobiles on U.S. roads in 1990 released, on the average, 96 percent less carbon monoxide than a quarter-century earlier.[12]

The matter seems pertinent in any effort to assess the nation's economic course through the rest of this century and beyond, and yet it seldom is raised: What sort of people are we Americans? As the 1990s unfold, beset by crime and the widespread use of illicit drugs, have we grown so soft after the post–World War II decades of high consumption and low productivity, of much borrowing and little saving, that we simply cannot mend our self-indulgent ways? Or, on a more optimistic note, are we tougher and more resilient than our political leadership has recognized, or the record of the Reagan years suggests, with the tax-rate cutting and mounting entitlements for the well-off? In this regard, it's worth noting that the average work week in America, at about forty hours, has lengthened by some two hours since the early Reagan years.

Much depends on how one chooses to approach such questions. The 1988 presidential race suggests a lack of fortitude. Recall the unhappy fate of Bruce Babbitt's campaign, after he was bold enough to suggest a national consumption tax. There was little stomach among the voters for any new tax, on consumption or on anything else, however sensible such a proposal may have been.

But there is a more encouraging way to gauge the willingness of Americans to face what Babbitt in his brief campaign called "reality." This is to consider in a somewhat different light the public response to the erosion of U.S. living standards that we have seen in recent years. The public's seeming acceptance of this erosion—and there will be more erosion to come—may reflect more than simply the power of Reagan's or Bush's political charm. It also can be seen as the response of people anxious to start addressing challenges made increasingly difficult by years of neglect, of a nation willing at last to begin to live *within* its means, for in the long run there is no other way.

This recognition was apparent in a survey in early 1990, when the dimensions of the S&L mess were becoming clearer. It found that two thirds of Americans advocated linking hourly pay increases to productivity gains. Eight of every ten, moreover, felt strongly that the government should spend more to train and educate the work force, and to this end, as well as to reduce the budget deficit, they were willing to pay more in federal taxes. In addition, 75 percent expressed concern that the U.S. economy was in a state of decline, relative to that of most other industrial nations. The survey concluded that Americans "are at last ready to take some strong medicine to deal with this crisis."[13] In June, California voters approved a boost in gasoline taxes and a higher ceiling on state spending, reversing the previous trend in the state. In New Jersey, meanwhile, the efforts of the new governor, James Florio, to put the state's fiscal house in order through a series of tax increases led Standard & Poor's Corp. in June to remove various New Jersey bond issues from the rating agency's "credit watch" list of securities being monitored for possible downgrading.

A crucial concern to ponder is not whether we Americans are at last ready and able to face up to the economic challenges that confront us, for we surely have that ability. The question is what will happen if we do not take action to pull ourselves back from an economic abyss caused by our self-indulgence. There are some people, as we have seen, who think deficits don't matter. But they do matter, and if we continue along our familiar course— allowing deficits and debt to pile up, neglecting domestic needs, continuing to pour money into dubious spending programs, refusing to set taxes at sufficient levels—then the outlook can only become increasingly bleak. Our position in global markets will continue to weaken. Foreign influence over our economy will continue to expand. Even as we go about the job of global policeman in the Middle East or elsewhere, the policing cost will drive up the budget deficit that foreigners help finance. More and more federal spending will be consumed simply in servicing the government's mounting debt. The dollar's international value will decline further, driving up the cost of foreign goods and services and cheapening the worth of U.S. goods and services, as well as of American real estate and factories.

There may be a way out of this predicament, but it has already been too long delayed. Taxes must be raised decisively and wasteful spending curbed, so as to reduce the budget deficit. But the reduction must be carried out with great care, so as not to shatter an already fragile economy. We do not have to erase the deficit in a matter of months. It would suffice merely to change the trajectory over the next few years—honestly, not with smoke and mirrors—from growth to shrinkage. Sacrifices will be required, and they will be painful, but if we fail to make them and continue to procrastinate, as we have done for so very long now, we will invite far deeper trouble. There is time to change our course, but there is dangerously little of it and still less of the courageous sort of leadership in Washington which the endeavor will demand.

H O P E springs eternal, but it is difficult in such circumstances to believe that very deep trouble can in fact be avoided. The economy has grown increasingly fragile after nearly a decade of expansion prolonged by the buildup of debt, mainly in the Reagan years. The business cycle remains intact, with a new recession bearing down the road. The Cold War peace dividend has gone east of Suez. To try to cut the budget deficit at such a recessionary time is hazardous, since reduced government spending and higher taxes act to restrain economic activity. That's hardly the formula for keeping a recession in check. Lower interest rates could help spur the economy, of course, but nowadays U.S. rate levels depend on decisions made in Tokyo or Frankfurt as well as at the Federal Reserve in Washington. Coming at a horrible time, the S&L debacle only worsens matters. As 1990 unfolded, the credit quality of American corporations was falling at a "record pace," according to Moody's Investors Service Inc.

Even if there were clear solutions to such economic problems, the political setting—at home as well as overseas—presents an obstacle. The political system, as we have seen, lacks flexibility. Each party wants the other to make the moves. Legislators who decry the deficit at the same time resist any effort to cut wasteful federal programs within their own areas. Leadership is missing.

As a nation, we have been partying, with such role models as Donald Trump. In a way, the whole country has been like Trump: Being rich was the fantasy of the 1980s, and Trump, best-selling author and casino entrepreneur, epitomized the dream. But now the party is over, and no one knows precisely how painful the developing hangover will turn out to be. It will be severe, a test of the nation's character. But it is not beyond our means to weather it and move on, through more sensible behavior to sounder prosperity.

NOTES

INTRODUCTION

1. Jacques Attali and others, "The Next World Order," interview, *New Perspectives Quarterly Journal,* Spring 1990.
2. Samuel P. Huntington, "The U.S.—Decline or Renewal?" *Foreign Affairs,* Winter 1988/89.
3. A survey by Harbour & Associates, reported in *Wall Street Journal,* Feb. 16, 1990.

CHAPTER ONE A DAUNTING NEW DECADE

1. George M. Woodwell, "Pollution, Erosion, Waste, Toxins," *New York Times,* Aug. 13, 1988.
2. John Yinger and Helen Ladd, *America's Ailing Cities* (Baltimore: Johns Hopkins University Press, 1989).
3. Study by the Conference Board, Jan. 27, 1989.
4. Survey by the Institute for Behavioral Research in Creativity of Salt Lake City, September 1989.
5. David D. Hale, "America in the Age of Japanese Financial Supremacy," paper, Kemper Financial Services Inc., January 1989.
6. Henry Kaufman, in *New York Times Sunday Magazine,* Oct. 9, 1988.
7. Atlanta Federal Reserve Bank, Economic Update of December 1988.
8. "Washington Wire," *Wall Street Journal,* Feb. 3, 1989.
9. *Grant's Interest Rate Observer,* Feb. 3, 1989.
10. Hale, "America in the Age of Japanese Financial Supremacy."
11. *Business Week,* Jan. 30, 1989.
12. Benjamin M. Friedman, *Day of Reckoning* (New York: Random House, 1988).

CHAPTER TWO A FADING DREAM

1. Brookings Institution, "American Living Standards," October 1988.
2. Milton Friedman, "Why the Twin Deficits Are a Blessing," editorial page, *Wall Street Journal,* Dec. 14, 1988.
3. Economic Policy Institute, "The State of Working America," Sept. 4, 1988.
4. *Economic Report of the President,* 1988.
5. *Business Week,* Aug. 29, 1988.
6. C. J. Lawrence, Morgan Grenfell Inc., "Weekly Economic Data," Jan. 18, 1988.
7. Committee for Economic Development, "New Dynamics in the Global Economy," October 1988.
8. Federal Reserve Bank of Atlanta, "Economic Review," August 1988.
9. Brown Brothers Harriman & Co., "International Comment," Feb. 12, 1988.
10. Bank of Tokyo study, March 1988.
11. Paul S. Hewitt, "Who Says We're Rich?" *Washington Post,* Jan. 3, 1989.
12. Economic Policy Institute, "The State of Working America," Sept. 4, 1988.
13. *Sound Advice* newsletter, March 1988.
14. David O. Maxwell, in *Washington Post,* Dec. 20, 1988.
15. Urban Institute report, Oct. 26, 1988.
16. Survey in *Time,* Oct. 10, 1988.
17. Vance Packard, *The Ultra Rich: How Much Is Too Much?* (Boston: Little, Brown, 1989).
18. *Washington Post,* March 9, 1989.
19. *New York Times,* Feb. 15, 1989.
20. Yearly data of the Department of Education and the American Council on Education.

CHAPTER THREE A TROUBLED LEGACY

1. M. S. Forbes, Jr., "How to Get Rid of the Budget Deficit," *Forbes,* May 29, 1989.
2. Robert Heilbroner and Peter Bernstein, *The Debt and the Deficit* (New York: W. W. Norton, 1989).
3. Robert Eisner, *How Real Is the Federal Deficit?* (New York: Free Press, 1986).
4. Institute for Research on the Economics of Taxation report, Feb. 7, 1989.
5. Jonathan Rauch, "Is the Deficit Really So Bad?" *Atlantic,* February 1989.
6. Nathaniel C. Nash, "No. 1 Whistle Blower Derides Deficit Figures," *New York Times,* April 24, 1989.
7. Peter G. Peterson and Neil Howe, *On Borrowed Time* (San Francisco: ICS Press, 1988).
8. BCA Publications Ltd., "Annual Report, U.S.A. Inc." March 1989.

9. Ben S. Bernanke and John Y. Campbell, "Is There a Corporate Debt Crisis?" Princeton University, Brookings Papers Number 1, 1988.

10. Paul A. Samuelson, *Economics,* 10th ed. (New York: McGraw-Hill, 1976).

11. "Perkin-Elmer Plans to Shed Unit," *New York Times,* April 22, 1989.

12. First Boston Corp., "Savings=Investment," economic commentary, Aug. 26, 1988.

13. 1985 Consumer Expenditure Interview Survey, Bureau of Labor Statistics.

14. Martin Feldstein, "A National Savings President," *Wall Street Journal,* Nov. 21, 1988.

15. *New York Motorist,* published by the Automobile Club of New York, March 1989.

16. Congressional Budget Office, "The Economic and Budget Outlook, Part 1," January 1989.

17. Burton A. Weisbrod, *The Nonprofit Economy* (Cambridge: Harvard University Press, 1988).

18. *Congressional Quarterly Weekly Report,* May 13, 1989.

19. Lloyd N. Cutler, "Pro-Life? Then Pay Up," *New York Times,* July 7, 1989.

20. Leon E. Panetta, "Who Will Pay for Bush's 'Vision'?" *Washington Post,* Aug. 3, 1989.

CHAPTER FOUR HARD TIMES

1. Fifty-state survey by Sindlinger & Co., Jan. 26, 1990.

2. Tax Foundation report, April 16, 1990.

3. John Markoff, "Corporate Lag in Research Funds," *New York Times,* Jan. 23, 1990.

4. Heritage Foundation, "A National Health System for America," June 1, 1989.

5. Robert L. DuPont and Ronald L. Goldfarb, "Drug Legalization: Asking for Trouble," *Washington Post,* Jan. 26, 1990. Dr. DuPont is a former director of the National Institute on Drug Abuse and Mr. Goldfarb is a former Justice Department prosecutor.

6. James Tobin, "A Case for Preserving Regulatory Distinctions," *Challenge,* November-December 1987.

7. Thomas M. Garrett, "Rotten from the Start," *Wall Street Journal,* Nov. 22, 1989.

8. Brookings Institution, "Road Work: A New Highway Pricing and Investment Policy," June 29, 1989.

9. Congressional Budget Office, "The Federal Deficit: Does It Measure the Government's Effect on Saving?" report, March 1990.

10. Subcommittee on Oversight and Investigations of the House Committee on Energy and Commerce, "Failed Promises: Insurance Company Insolvencies," report, February 1990.

CHAPTER FIVE LAGGING LEADERS

1. *Business Week*/Harris Poll, reported in *Business Week*, Aug. 7, 1989.
2. Jill Abramson and Eduardo Lachica, "Familiar Faces," *Wall Street Journal*, Feb. 23, 1990.
3. Poll by *The Wall Street Journal* and NBC News, reported in *Wall Street Journal*, April 20, 1990.
4. Janice Castro, "Working Scared," *Time*, Sept. 11, 1989.
5. *National Law Journal* survey, Feb. 21, 1989.
6. Survey by Yankelovich Clancy Shulman, reported in *Time*, Nov. 13, 1989.
7. Phil Gramm and Warren B. Rudman, "We Made a Commitment," *New York Times*, Oct. 25, 1989.
8. Dan Rostenkowski, "Gramm-Rudman? Let the Ax Fall," *New York Times*, Oct. 13, 1989.

CHAPTER SIX LOOKING AHEAD

1. Estimates by Robert Kutscher, associate commissioner of the Bureau of Labor Statistics, quoted in *New York Times*, April 15, 1990.
2. Eric Schmitt, "Our Towns," column, *New York Times*, April 20, 1990.
3. Edward Yardeni with Amalia Quintana, *The Baby Boom Chart Book*, (Prudential-Bache Securities Inc., 1989).
4. Congressional Budget Office, "Reducing the Deficit: A Report to the Senate and House Committees on the Budget—Part II," February 1989.
5. Andy Ireland, "A Hawk Says: Pull Out Our Troops," *New York Times*, March 7, 1989.
6. *New York Times*/CBS News telephone poll of 1,140 adults, reported in *New York Times*, May 27, 1990.
7. C. Fred Bergsten, statement to the House Budget Committee, Jan. 25, 1989.
8. George N. Hatsopoulos, "Saving Decline Wasn't Just the Deficit," *Wall Street Journal*, May 4, 1989.
9. Survey by Louis Harris & Associates, reported in *Business Week*, April 16, 1990.
10. Gallup Poll, released by the National Federation of Independent Business, Jan. 11, 1990.
11. "Economic Prospects for the Year 2000," *Business Week*, Sept. 25, 1989.
12. Conference Board, "U.S. Environmental Progress," April 20, 1990.
13. Survey by Louis Harris & Associates, reported by Louis Harris in *New York Times*, May 23, 1990.

INDEX

ABOUT THE AUTHOR

ALFRED L. MALABRE, JR., is a columnist and editor at *The Wall Street Journal* as well as the author of five earlier books, including *Beyond Our Means,* published in 1987, which was awarded the Eccles Prize as the year's best book in the field of economics by Columbia University's Graduate School of Business. He began his career in journalism at the *Hartford Courant,* after four years in the U.S. Navy and after work at Columbia's School of Journalism. He joined *The Wall Street Journal* in 1958 and has served as a correspondent for the paper in Chicago and London, as its Bonn bureau chief, and as a reporter and then as economic news editor and "Outlook" columnist in New York City, where he resides. He is a graduate of Yale University.